T0419536

# BUILDING STRATEGIC LANGUAGE ABILITY PROGRAMS

# LANGUAGES AND LINGUISTICS SERIES

**Critical Discourse Analysis: An Interdisciplinary Perspective**
*Thao Le, Quynh Le and Megan Short (Editors)*
2009. ISBN: 978-1-60741-320-2

**Critical Discourse Analysis: An Interdisciplinary Perspective**
*Thao Le, Quynh Le and Megan Short (Editors)*
2009. ISBN: 978-1-60876-772-4 (Online Book)

**Building Language Skills and Cultural Competencies in the Military**
*Edgar D. Swain (Editor)*
2009. ISBN: 978-1-60741-126-0

**Building Language Skills and Cultural Competencies in the Military**
*Edgar D. Swain (Editor)*
2009. ISBN: 978-1-60876-597-3 (Online Book)

**Second Languages: Teaching, Learning and Assessment**
*Ryan L. Jikal and Samantha A. Raner (Editors)*
2009. ISBN: 978-1-60692-661-1

**Aphasia: Symptoms, Diagnosis and Treatment**
*Grigore Ibanescu and Serafim Pescariu (Editors)*
2009. ISBN: 978-1-60741-288-5

**Building Strategic Language Ability Programs**
*Joshua R. Weston (Editor)*
2010. ISBN: 978-1-60741-127-7

LANGUAGES AND LINGUISTICS SERIES

# BUILDING STRATEGIC LANGUAGE ABILITY PROGRAMS

**Joshua R. Weston**
**Editor**

Nova Science Publishers, Inc.
New York

### NOTICE TO THE READER

The Publisher has taken reasonable care in the preparation of this book, but makes no expressed or implied warranty of any kind and assumes no responsibility for any errors or omissions. No liability is assumed for incidental or consequential damages in connection with or arising out of information contained in this book. The Publisher shall not be liable for any special, consequential, or exemplary damages resulting, in whole or in part, from the readers' use of, or reliance upon, this material. Any parts of this book based on government reports are so indicated and copyright is claimed for those parts to the extent applicable to compilations of such works.

Independent verification should be sought for any data, advice or recommendations contained in this book. In addition, no responsibility is assumed by the publisher for any injury and/or damage to persons or property arising from any methods, products, instructions, ideas or otherwise contained in this publication.

This publication is designed to provide accurate and authoritative information with regard to the subject matter covered herein. It is sold with the clear understanding that the Publisher is not engaged in rendering legal or any other professional services. If legal or any other expert assistance is required, the services of a competent person should be sought. FROM A DECLARATION OF PARTICIPANTS JOINTLY ADOPTED BY A COMMITTEE OF THE AMERICAN BAR ASSOCIATION AND A COMMITTEE OF PUBLISHERS.

LIBRARY OF CONGRESS CATALOGING-IN-PUBLICATION DATA

Building strategic language ability programs / editor, Joshua R. Weston.
    p. cm.
  Includes index.
  ISBN 978-1-60741-127-7 (hardcover)
  1.  Language and languages--Ability testing. 2.  Communicative competence.  I. Weston, Joshua R.
  P53.4.B85 2009
  428.0076--dc22
               2009028447

*Published by Nova Science Publishers, Inc.* ✦ *New York*

# CONTENTS

# PREFACE

This book explores the consensus that has emerged that the American education system must more aggressively embrace the concept of global education for a broader population of students. The products of American education generally remain woefully unprepared to engage in a rapidly changing socio-economic and political environment that demands global skills. This book examines the most needed of these skills, which is the ability to effectively engage in languages other than English. Since its inception in 2000, the Department of Defense Language Flagship Initiative has provided important funding to the American higher education system to re-tool its approaches to language education. At the core of the Flagship concept is the assumption that the development of global skills (including advanced language competency) must be mainstreamed into American education. As this book discusses, any approach to achieving language competency must ultimately begin as early as pre-school, middle school, and high school.

Chapter 1 – This chapter is comprised of the statement of the Oversight and Investigations Subcommittee during the hearing on the DOD's Work with States, Universities, and Students to Transform the Nation's Foreign Language Capacity, September 23, 2008

Chapter 2: This chapter is comprised of the statement of Galal Walker, National East Asian Languages Resource Center, The Ohio State University, before the House Armed Services Committee, Subcommittee on Oversight and Investigations, dated September 23, 2008

Chapter 3: This chapter is comprised of the statement of Terri E. Givens, University of Texas at Austin, before the House Armed Services Committee, Subcommittee on Oversight and Investigations, dated September 23, 2008

Chapter 4: This chapter is comprised of the statement of Robert O. Slater, National Security Education Program, before the House Armed Services Committee, Subcommittee on Oversight and Intelligence, dated September 23, 2008

Chapter 5: This chapter is comprised of the statement of Dana S. Bourgerie, the National Chinese Flagship Center at Brigham Young University, before the House Armed Services Committee, Subcommittee on Oversight and Investigations, dated September 23, 2008

In: Building Strategic Language Ability Programs
Editor: Joshua R. Weston

ISBN: 978-1-60741-127-7
© 2009 Nova Science Publishers, Inc.

*Chapter 1*

# STATEMENT OF OVERSIGHT AND INVESTIGATIONS SUBCOMMITTEE: HEARING ON THE DOD'S WORK WITH STATES, UNIVERSITIES, AND STUDENTS TO TRANSFORM THE NATION'S FOREIGN LANGUAGE CAPACITY

## *Vic Snyder*

September 23, 2008

"The hearing will come to order. Good morning, and welcome to the Subcommittee on Oversight and Investigations' hearing on the goals and directions of Department of Defense efforts to improve its language and cultural awareness capabilities.

"Today's session is the third in a series of hearings examining efforts to improve the foreign language, cultural awareness, and regional expertise capabilities of United States general purpose military forces. Witnesses at both of the previous hearings noted that the U.S. population is generally marked by a lack of foreign language skills, a notable exception being those skills found in recent immigrant communities. They also noted the long neglect and decline of foreign language emphasis in the American education system at all levels.

"This third hearing addresses federal and state programs, including DOD's, intention to mitigate, if not reverse, that national decline. I hope that after hearing from the witnesses, we'll have a better idea of how to improve our K-12 educational system and higher education in order to increase the nation's competitiveness and meet the foreign language proficiency needs of the Defense Department and other government agencies for national security.

"The key programs we'll be discussing today include:

- DOD's National Security Education Program (NSEP);
- The Interagency National Security Language Initiative (NLSI);
- The National Language Service Corps (NLSC);
- The Flagship Program; and

- The State Language Education Roadmaps or Strategies.

"We are joined today by:

- Dr. Robert Slater, who joined the National Security Education Program in 1992 and has served as its director since 1996. Dr. Slater had a key role in the development of both the Language Flagship and the National Language Service Corps. As the Director of NSEP, he also serves on the National Security Education Board.
- Dr. Terri E. Givens is the Frank C. Erwin, Jr. Centennial Honors Professor and Vice Provost at the University of Texas at Austin. Texas-Austin is one of three Arabic Flagship Centers and is also the sole Hindi/Urdu Flagship Center.
- Dr. Dana Bourgerie is an Associate Professor of Chinese and the Director of the Chinese Flagship Center at Brigham Young University. His research interests include dialect studies, and he has published an article on computer-aided learning for Chinese.
- Dr. Galal Walker is Professor of Chinese and Director, National East Asian Languages Resource Center and Chinese Flagship Center at Ohio State University. Ohio State University, along with Brigham Young University, is one of four Chinese Flagship Centers.

In: Building Strategic Language Ability Programs
Editor: Joshua R. Weston

ISBN: 978-1-60741-127-7
© 2010 Nova Science Publishers, Inc.

*Chapter 2*

# Statement of Galal Walker, National East Asian Languages Resource Center, The Ohio State University, before the House Armed Services Committee, Subcommittee on Oversight and Investigations

## Introduction

Chairman, Vic Snyder, members of this distinguished committee, and your special guest, Congressman Rush Holt, I am grateful and for the opportunity to speak on the role we in Ohio are playing in the national effort to prepare our country for the interdependent global community of the 21$^{st}$ Century. We are primarily motivated by the successes of our students, who have shown time and again that young Americans can reach the highest level of foreign language and culture expertise if given the right opportunities and resources. We see the mission of the Ohio State University Chinese Flagship Center as preparing young Americans to succeed in careers that involve extended interactions with counterparts in China and the interpretation of the intentions of Chinese individuals and organizations. Graduates of our program are prepared to work with Chinese counterparts and organizations to achieve commonly understood goals.

**Chinese Flagship Center:** Our Center at Ohio State is undertaking four programs that advance our mission: 1) The Chinese Flagship, which focuses on bringing students to the highest levels of proficiency and communicative skills within Chinese culture; 2) the K-12 Chinese Flagship Program, which works to provide schools across Ohio with he capacity to effectively teach Chinese; 3) Flagship Center in Qingdao, which currently manages in-China internships and summer programs; and 4) The Language Summit and *Ohio Language Roadmap for the 21st Century*.

In order to carry out the mission of our Center, we have adopted three strategies to guide our operations: 1) Teach language in culture, 2) Combine language with content knowledge, 3) Utilize technology, and 4) Assess performance. In the following paragraphs, I will expand on these strategies and, when I describe the programs later, I will explain how each program implements these four strategies.

## Teach Language in Culture

The assumption that the purpose of these programs is to produce demonstrable abilities to communicate in Chinese requires us to explicitly frame language instruction in Chinese culture. I try to alert every Chinese language student that cultural understanding is absolutely necessary to their future success by warning them: "If you want to speak Chinese the way you speak English, you can learn to do that since you all are obviously talented in language learning. It will take you five to seven years of demanding and persistent work. After all that, you will have only gained the ability to immediately annoy 1.3 billion people." To assure that our students are not annoying to the Chinese and can more accurately interpret Chinese intentions, we build into our materials and practices communication frames that reflect the social expectations of Chinese culture. At the beginning levels, for example, we teach learners of Chinese to present and refer to themselves as members of a group rather than as individuals; at the advanced levels, we create opportunities to engage in in-depth studies of topics from the Chinese perspective, making sure that our students are familiar what most of their Chinese counterparts know about a commonly known subject. We have a course entitled "Chinese Perspectives on China's Civilization" that is taught by established Chinese academics serving as visiting scholars who regularly expose our students to important ideas and viewpoints that are not encountered in the classes of Western academics. We tell our students that our goal is to make them appear intelligent in Chinese culture and key to giving that impression is a demonstrable knowledge of Chinese culture and the ability to express explicit respect for the culture.

Regardless whether American students of Chinese will use their linguistic skills and knowledge with Chinese people in interactions, transactions, presentations, or interpretation, being familiar with the experiences and expectations of their counterparts in China is crucial. Such knowledge is only gained through a persistent and prolonged exposure to and performance of Chinese cultural norms.

## Combine Language with Selected Content Knowledge

Adult learners of the language do not learn Chinese; they learn to *do things* in Chinese. The more things they can do in Chinese, the more expert they are in the language. Since the language and culture is too immense to "learn" as a whole, students and teachers have to restrict the targets to areas that will be most useful and most needed as the students' Chinese learning careers develop.

As a program, we have to choose the *things* that a learner will learn to do in Chinese. The better we are at choosing and implementing this instruction, the more efficient the learning and teaching become.

At the higher levels of instruction, students combine their language study with what we call "domain study." A domain is either an academic field or a career area and the ability to combine domains with an intensive program of Chinese is one of the great advantages of our location at a large public institution. With OSU's extensive international community of students, faculty, and staff, almost any academic interest can be matched with a native speaker who is eager to assist young Americans in their pursuit of advanced skills in Chinese.

Our students have chosen a wide variety of domains: among them, microfinance, public health, marketing, emerging political and economic forces in China, and even real estate.

At the elementary and middle school levels of Chinese study, after inculcating the foundation skills of listening, speaking, reading, and composition, we are focusing the Chinese lessons on subjects in natural science. After reaching intermediate or ILR level 1, we will introduce a progression of materials in mathematics, astronomy, biology, geography, and environmental studies. We have pedagogical reasons for this direction: Chinese vocabulary in the natural sciences is more transparent than the English terminology. Thus, as students are increasing their skills in the language, they reinforce basic science skills. Secondly, since we intend to eventually hook Ohio classrooms up with classrooms in China, the natural science subject mater will give our students a shareable frame of discussion and presentation.

## Utilize Technology

We are in the process of catching our pedagogy up to the technological resources available to us. Over the past decade and a half, we have gained the ability to show language learners naturally occurring communication events, connect them to native speaking counterparts at almost any point on the globe, and link different kinds of information that can be accessed any where at any time. Our Challenge is to render all of these opportunities for our students in the most effective ways. While we are making progress on this front, we still have a long way to go to realize the full potential.

At the beginning level, we expose students to short video recordings of Chinese communicating with each other and then coach them through the events so they can understand them, replicate them, and participate in similar events, essentially increasing our students' sophistication in the language by steadily increasing the number of communication events in which they can successfully participate. On the advanced levels, we provide broadcast programming with coordinated scripts to exercise listening and extensive sets of examples of video clips showing specific events (e.g., refusing, complimenting, and taking leave). To facilitate extensive reading, we put native texts online and combine them with audio programs, search and concordance functions, and electronic reference systems. With the expanding video-conferencing capacities, we create events such as thesis events that include audience and participants in both Columbus, Ohio and Qingdao, China.

## Assess Performance

Effective language learning requires a prolonged experience of performing the language in meaningful contexts. Assuring the effectiveness of the instruction requires us to assess our students' performances throughout their learning career. To this end, we have developed an online e-portfolio, Advanced Language Performance Portfolio System (ALPPS), to provide a longitudinal record of our students' progress in the language. Using "You Tube-type" technology student performances of key interactions (e.g., conversation, presentation) are collected in individual and class files, which are then subject to evaluation by teachers and native speakers with pedagogical or domain expertise. This provides us with extensive sets of transparent evaluations—meaning that students, teachers, and eventually recruiters can view the evaluation reports, identify the groups of evaluators, and drill down to the actual events on which the evaluations are based.

Our program goals are stated in terms of proficiency standards, namely the Interagency Language Roundtable (ILR) proficiency ratings. The highest level of programming is focused on producing ILR 3 and above. We view proficiency as a summative assessment and do not train our students to sit for proficiency examinations. Rather we assume that a regimen of accurate evaluations of well-chosen performances will lead to solid performances on the standard proficiency examinations. In addition to the ILR and ACTFL proficiency assessments, ALPPS also records and tracks performances on standardized tests such as the Chinese Ministry of Education HSK and our own Chinese Computer-Adaptive Listening Test and Chinese Computer-Adaptive Reading tests.

Our programs include internships where our students spend time in Chinese workplaces, contributing to the goals of the host organizations and working cooperatively with Chinese colleagues. This experience has brought about a revelation of the shortcomings of American assessments of foreign language capacities. That is, we train our students in Chinese and then we assess their (and our) achievements by testing them with instruments that we devise without reference to the opinion of non-English speaking native- speaker members of Chinese culture.

When ILR or ACTFL proficiency ratings consistently seemed to be poor indicators of our interns' success in Chinese work environments, it became clear that Chinese organizations and individuals were looking for abilities that were not reflected in these tests. Therefore, we have begun to place emphasis on recruiting evaluators for ALPPS performance files from China and launching research projects to discover what native speakers of Chinese in the workplace see as beneficial in the communication efforts of our students.

## Challenges Facing the OSU Chinese Flagship Center

We are continuing to work toward making advanced language training the standard for our institutions. This requires us to find ways to shift the focus from *teaching* Chinese to *learning* Chinese. This seemingly slight change of perspective seems to challenge the way we run our schools. We need to encourage more investment in advanced language training, making sure that we can provide adequate opportunities to all the students who seek to pursue excellence in this field. We need to lower barriers between our classrooms and the institutions in which our students will have to make their livelihoods. Finally, we need to find a way to secure facilities in China where we can continue to serve our students. Having our own facilities will keep our costs more constant in an environment that is quickly becoming more expensive, following the pattern in other areas of East Asia. Finally, we need to keep track of our students after they leave our programs. These young people comprise an incredible resource for our programs, society, and Nation just as long as we know how to contact them.

# CHINESE FLAGSHIP PROGRAM

This program has permitted us to raise the standard for Chinese language study at Ohio State. By building the Chinese Flagship around a Master's of Arts that is earned by attaining ILR level 3 (tested by FSI or ACTFL, whose designation is "superior") in speaking and reading, completing a thesis written and defended in Chinese, and publicly demonstrating an ability to give presentations in and discuss a domain (i.e., academic major or occupational area), language and culture proficiency has been instituted as the standard for learning and teaching achievement. The Ohio State Chinese Flagship is a two-year program. The first academic year is spent in Columbus, taking courses delivered completely in Chinese. The subjects are chosen to prepare the students to function in formal social environments: China's media, networking in China and the United States, Literary language in modern mandarin, Language in China, Chinese perspectives on China's civilization, and Negotiation in China. These courses are taught by native speakers that include visiting scholars recruited from universities and companies in China. We also assign a mentor for each student based on his or her declared domain and the two works together in an individualized instruction course to develop a research agenda that will eventually lead to a thesis. Mentors are recruited from the Central Ohio Chinese community and include graduate students, faculty, and staff from Ohio State as well as professionals outside the university. In every course, the students are required to deal with textual materials from China, engage in class discussions, take tests that reflect Chinese testing procedures, and give presentations of their individual research.

One indication that the first year of this program is effective is the record of our students in the Chinese Bridge, an annual international competition in Chinese language proficiency sponsored by China's Ministry of Education. This contest involves well over 100 students of Chinese as a foreign language who have won regional competitions in over 50 countries. Our students participate in the US regional competition and the final contest in China, which is televised throughout China. This occurs during the summer between the first and second year in the OSU Flagship Program. In the past five years students, from Ohio State have earned three first place, one second place, and two third place awards in the international competition in China and fourteen first, second, and third place awards at the regional level in New York City. No other college or university has approached this record of achievement.

More impressive is the performance of these students in their internship assignments, which constitute about one-half of their second year in China. Our students spend months working in Chinese organizations more often than not as the only non-Chinese staff. The internships are arranged and supervised by the program, with the resident director in China keeping track of their work and monitoring the host organization's satisfaction. To the present, Flagship students from OSU and BYU have worked in 29 organizations in China, including serving as a program assistant in the China International Economic and Trade Arbitration Commission (CIETAC), researching intellectual property rights in a Shanghai law firm, and working on production teams for China Central Television. With proper preparation, the experience of working successfully within a Chinese organization leads to a rapid gain in language and an irreversible gain in confidence.

The OSU Chinese Flagship Program has attracted a rather wide demographic range of young Americans who are willing to devote their time and energy to the pursuit of advanced skills in Chinese. The first three cohorts of Flagship students consisted of 26 students from 18 states and 20 different universities with 15 different undergraduate majors. Our students are 89% non-heritage and 69% male. NSEP fellowships supported 39% of the students with program and department support going to 44% and 17% being self-supporting.

Beginning in 2007, the program included undergraduate students. Initially undergraduates were "combined degree" students, being enrolled in an undergraduate BA or BS degree program and a Chinese MA program at the same time. For exceptionally performing students, this permits earning the undergraduate and graduate degrees concurrently. But, for most it allows the student to earn the MA one year after obtaining the BA or BS. In the most recent cohorts, we have undergraduates who qualify for Flagship courses before graduating. In the 2008 cohort about one half of the Flagship students have undergraduate status. In coming years, we intend to expand the undergraduate element by recruiting students who begin their undergraduate career with intermediate to advanced skills in Chinese. This leads us to a discriminating set of terms: Flagship Fellow, for NSEP funded students who enroll full time in Flagship courses; Flagship scholars who are other-funded and full-time in Flagship courses; Flagship students, who qualify for at least one Flagship course and have at least two majors; and Flagship preps, who are on track to reaching advanced Chinese as undergraduates.

## K-12 CHINESE FLAGSHIP

With China emerging on the global stage and growing Ohio exports to China increasing ($1.5 billion in 2007), Chinese language has finally caught the attention of secondary and even elementary schools throughout Ohio. In 2006, only a few schools in Ohio offered Chinese language instruction. Because of the joint efforts of schools and districts, the OSU K-12 Chinese Flagship Program and Ohio Department of Education (ODE), K-12 Chinese has witnessed a significant growth in Ohio schools. The number of schools and students engaged in Chinese studies in the 2007-08 school year almost tripled over the previous year. Here we will describe the current conditions of K-12 Chinese in Ohio and future plans of the OSU K-12 Flagship program's partnership with K-12 schools to offer innovative and effective Chinese programs.

**The OSU K-12 Chinese Flagship Program:** The OSU K-12 Chinese Flagship Program has worked closely with Ohio Department of Education in many areas, including co-hosting two statewide conferences on K-12 Chinese in December of 2006 and 2007. The program goal is to build the infrastructure for Ohio schools to establish successful language programs leading to solid communication skills in Mandarin Chinese. The program is developing partnerships in Ohio and beyond to achieve objectives that include the following:

- Developing a multi-access, performance-based curriculum;
- Providing teacher support and ongoing professional development; and
- Creating a technology support system with effective Chinese language programs.

Our current stage of K-12 curriculum development consists of two sets of materials: 1) a 9-12 introduction entitled *Chinese: Communicating in the Culture* which includes an interactive DVD, a textbook, and a MP3 audio program; and 2) a P-5 set of materials designed to be implemented in three *phases* followed by a series of language materials dealing with natural science topics. The phases are designed to be offered in a manner analogous to beginning, intermediate, and advance orchestra, where beginning students can start the study of the language at Phase I and work their way through the remaining phases by demonstrating command of performance standards. This permits multiple points of access to a program and avoids the necessity to progress in the language on a grade-by-grade basis. Completing Phase III will give the students a firm foundation in listening, speaking, and a solid introduction to the writing system. From that point, we will provide language instruction that focuses on science-related topics: mathematics, astronomy, biology, geography, chemistry and environmental science. We have three reasons for choosing this direction for our curriculum: 1) Chinese science vocabulary is more transparent than English, e.g., volcano is *huo-shan* "fire-mountain" and glacier is *bing-he* "ice-river"; thus, Chinese can reinforce subjects studied in English. 2) We intend to connect our classrooms with classrooms in China and feel that natural science subject matter will be both easier and more attractive as a mutually accessible field of communication for both our students and Chinese students. 3) We can avoid the issues of cultural relativity that seems to be difficult for middle-school-aged students to cope with, leaving the more culturally oriented subject to high school and/or summer intensive language camps.

The OSU K-12 Chinese Flagship Program is interested in supporting any school in Ohio that is operating or plans to start a Chinese language program. We are building partnerships with a select number of schools to create model Chinese programs for Ohio schools. We are also working on creating partnerships with corporations, heritage schools and other public and private entities to generate creative support for the development of K-12 Chinese in Ohio and beyond. Ultimately, we want to see more Ohio students to be proficient in Chinese language and knowledgeable about Chinese life and culture. This will not only eventually broaden our students' career possibilities and benefit Ohio's economy, but also improve our national security and international relations.

## K-12 Chinese Programs in Ohio

According to data collected by the OSU K-12 Chinese Flagship Program, the number of Ohio schools and districts offering Chinese language has increased from 8 three years ago to 50 in the 2007-08 school year (Exhibit 1). Meanwhile, the number of students enrolled in Chinese increased from 777 (ODE data) in 2006-07 to more than 2,000 in regular language programs (offering 3-10 sessions each week) in the current school year. In addition, more than 3,000 elementary and middle school students are enrolled in Chinese exploration programs, offering 1-2 sessions each week (Exhibit 2). More high school students are learning Chinese through distance learning and the OSU summer programs for college credits and/or high school credits.

## The Growth of Chinese Programs in Ohio Schools, 2005–06 to 2007–08

The sharp increase of Chinese programs and student enrollment in the last two years is the result of joint efforts of school/district administrators, OSU K-12 Chinese Flagship

Program and ODE. The biggest increase occurred in the last two years, especially after we co-hosted the conference in December 2006, titled "Making the Global Connections: Linking Students and China in the 21st Century."

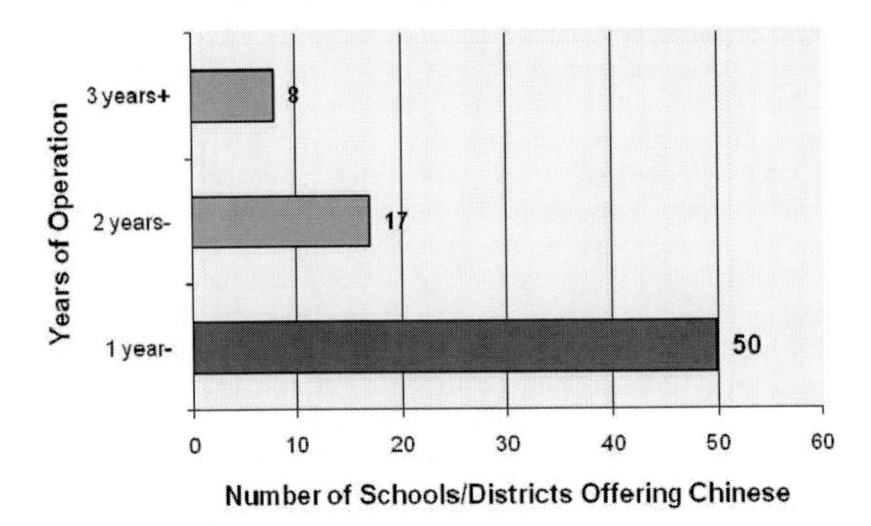

**Number of Schools/Districts Offering Chinese**

**Range of Ohio Schools Offering Chinese:** The Ohio K-12 schools offering Chinese are concentrated in and around metropolitan areas (Appendices A&B), but they represent a wide range:

- Public (including charter or community) and private schools (14 private schools consisting of 27% of the total number of schools with Chinese programs); and
- Urban, suburban and rural schools. (The new Chinese language programs starting in the 2008-09 school year seem to follow this pattern.)
- There is also a wide variety of ways Chinese language instruction is delivered:
- Classroom instruction (for most schools and districts);
- Distance learning for students at multiple sites (e.g., Diocese of Columbus);
- Distance learning of individualized instruction for college credits (e.g., OSU);
- Summer programs: Regents' Chinese Academy (funded by State of Ohio, with 50 high school students last year and another 50 this summer) and Chinese Immersion Summer Day Camps (funded by StarTalk and operated at three sites: Cleveland, Columbus, and Dayton, with more than 70 students);
- Exploration learning for special education students (e.g., Summit Academy Schools);
- Full language programs (3-10 sessions per week, usually in high schools) vs. exploration programs (1-2 sessions per week, usually in elementary schools).

Distance learning may be a solution to rural schools where some students want to take Chinese but the numbers are not big enough for schools to hire teachers. Currently, the Diocese of Columbus is using videoconferencing equipment (Polycom) to offer Chinese to 6th graders in eight urban and rural schools. The OSU K-12 Chinese Flagship Program is providing distance learning of individualized instruction and is providing a distance learning pilot to 12 students in Dover High School in eastern Ohio.

In addition to the traditional K-12 schools, an important provider of Chinese language and culture to children and adults during weekends is the heritage schools in all Ohio metropolitan areas (e.g., Ohio Contemporary Chinese School in Columbus, Cincinnati Contemporary Chinese School, Chinese Academy of Cleveland, Cleveland Contemporary Chinese School in Solon City, the Greater Dayton Chinese School, and Toledo Chinese School). Some of these schools have a large enrollment--up to 500 students. The majority of students are from heritage families, but increasingly, non-heritage students are signing up, particularly those from organizations like Families with Children from China (FCC). Most of the heritage schools are members of a national Chinese School Association in the United States (CSAUS). The OSU K-12 Chinese Flagship Program is working closely with some of the heritage schools. For example, we partner with them to operate the Chinese Immersion Summer Day Camps in three Ohiometro areas: Cleveland, Columbus, and Dayton.

**Type of Students Learning Chinese in K-12 Schools:** The majority of the Ohio students are taking Chinese as exploratory courses in K-8 programs. That means they spend only one or two sessions a week and some schools only offer exploratory Chinese for a part of one school year. This is certainly not the direction we should promote for learning Mandarin Chinese. We are keeping track of these exploratory programs to learn whether or not they lead to more serious goals. All high school students (29% of total enrollment), however, are taking Chinese as a regular language program, most of them taking classes every day.

The other challenge of fast growing Chinese programs is to maintain program quality. Nearly all the students (95%) are beginners. This demonstrates that sustaining programs and keeping students continuously interested in learning Chinese are important tasks. This is why we made "program maintenance" an important component of the annual conference in December 2007. This will be given even more attention when we plan for the third annual conference for December 2008.

**An Initial Assessment of Teachers of Chinese:** The significant growth of K-12 Chinese programs in Ohio presents great opportunities for us, but it also creates tremendous challenges, particularly in the areas of teacher and curriculum development. The OSU K-12 Chinese Flagship Program is developing its capacities and has worked with partners to meet these challenges.

Ohio has done a relatively good job in preparing certified teachers of Chinese for K-12 schools, thanks to state funding and the Chinese teacher licensure programs at three universities (OSU, Cleveland State, and Akron). In the last school year, 24 Chinese language teachers graduated from the OSU licensure program and 16 from the CSU program. Some of these teachers were already teaching Chinese in the K-12 schools, and about half have found teaching positions. However, some have not been hired to teach Chinese because they are not willing to relocate to where the jobs are. Therefore, future Chinese teacher licensure training programs should take relocation issue into consideration. Ohio still has some teachers who are not licensed, most of whom are in private schools. The guest teachers sent from China meet the temporary licensure requirement set by ODE. But a licensed teacher does not mean that s/he is automatically more effective than other teachers. Guest teachers from China who are made available to schools at no or little cost causes some difficulty in finding positions for the teachers we certify. This will require attention in the future as we seek to establish Chinese language study as a permanent presence in Ohio schools.

According to school visits, class observations and teacher professional development workshops in the last year and half, it seems all teachers of Chinese are dedicated and excited about their new jobs and the overall development of Chinese programs in Ohio. However, most of them, including those holding teaching licenses, lack sufficient pedagogical training to help American students to learn Chinese language effectively. For example, most teachers speak too much English in class, including often repeated basic classroom instructions. The students are doing too much translation in the classroom rather than performing what they learn in Chinese cultural contexts. We intend to provide more support to the newly formed Ohio Association of Teachers of Chinese and more professional development opportunities for the teachers to deal with this problem.

## Number of K-12 Chinese Language Teachers in Ohio (Total: 57), 2007–08

The above number (57) of teachers does not include those in heritage schools, which only operate on weekends and focus on heritage children. It does not include the two guest teachers from the Confucius Institutes in the state. The 21 guest teachers in Ohio schools include 19 sponsored by Hanban or other Chinese organizations, two hired by the Teachers of Critical Language Program (TCLP, funded by the State Department), and one from Taiwan. In the next school year, there will be 23 Hanban guest teachers coming to Ohio schools (most of them replacing the current teachers), five of whom will start new Chinese programs in the schools or districts they are placed. There will also be more TCLP teachers from China and more from Taiwan.

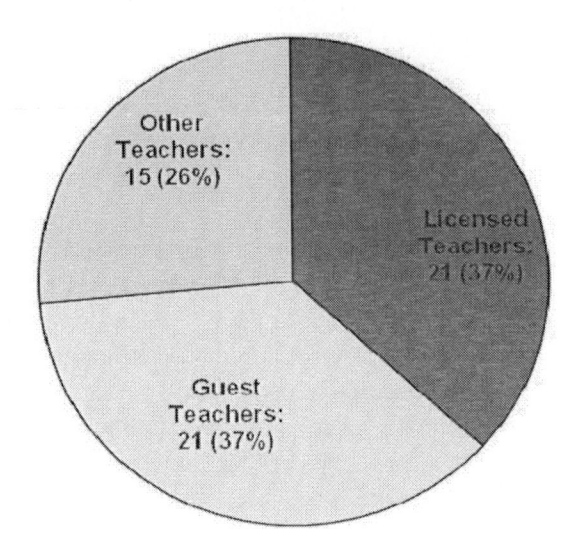

The guest teacher program is a big help to some schools that want to start a Chinese program but are temporarily short of funds, or for those that want to add to their existing Chinese programs. However, the guest teacher program is temporary in nature; schools and districts should not regard it as a permanent solution and rely on it for long-term program development. Although the guest teachers are intelligent and increasingly well trained, they have unique challenges. For example, most of them are not familiar with teaching Chinese as a foreign language (their training background is at best "teaching Chinese as a second language"); most of them return to their home country after one year of teaching, thus creating uncertainty for schools and students; and some schools have encountered management and cultural difficulties with guest teachers that have led to eliminating their entire Chinese program (e.g., Belpre Schools).

**Teacher Development:** Ohio is taking the lead in training Chinese language teachers. The State has invested money since September 2006 to operate year-long Chinese licensure programs at OSU, Cleveland State, and University of Akron. (The contact information is: Dr. Charles Hancock of OSU at hancock.2@osu.edu, Dr. Jane Ann Zaharias of CSU at J.ZAHARIAS@csuohio.edu, and Dr. Susan Colville Hall of UA at colvill@usakron.edu.) The first group of 40 teachers of Chinese graduated last summer, and the second group will graduate by the end of this summer.

The OSU Department of East Asian Languages and Literature (DEALL) has operated a Chinese language teacher training program for over a decade: Summer Program of East Asian Concentration, or SPEAC. It is an intensive seven-week program offering 15 graduate credits. It focuses on pedagogical training and the trainees have hands-on experience with high school students who are taking Chinese during the summer. The program director is Dr. Mari Noda, the chairperson of DEALL. For more information about SPEAC, please visit http://deall.osu.edu/programs/summerPrgm.

The OSU K-12 Chinese Flagship Program has provided four one-day teacher development workshops in Columbus and Cleveland in the past twelve months. The workshops focus on creating Chinese environments in the classroom and performance-based pedagogical issues. The formal (written evaluation) and informal feedback indicates that teachers were satisfied with the professional development and the training helped them in their teaching. We are planning to provide more teacher development workshops in the near future, including more intensive workshop for partner school teachers and workshop during the OATC annual meeting. We also plan to create a webpage on the K-12 Chinese Flagship website for teachers to connect and share resources.

In addition to the regular year-long Chinese teacher licensure program provided by OSU, the K-12 Chinese Flagship Program provides information to help teachers who are already teaching Chinese in a K-12 school but cannot participate in the year-long program to apply for an alternative educator license.

**The Ohio Model: Innovations for Effective Programs:** The goals of the NSEP funded Language Flagship programs for critical languages are innovation and effectiveness, and then diffusion of the innovations. (For more information about The Language Flagship programs nationally, please visit http://www.thelanguageflagship.org). The OSU K-12 Chinese Flagship Program is less than three years old, but it has significantly impacted the development of Chinese language programs in Ohio schools. Unlike the Oregon K-12 Chinese program, which is focused on a partial immersion model within one school district, the Ohio model has a statewide approach, providing technical assistance to any school that operates or plans to offer Chinese language programs. Meanwhile, we work with a selected number of "partner schools" to develop model programs. We have six partner schools in the

Cleveland, Columbus and Dayton metropolitan areas. We intend to add three more partner schools every year, schools selected to engage in more collaborative work. Eventually we intend to connect the Chinese classrooms in partner schools and with schools in China via the Internet.

By working with schools and partners, we strive to meet the needs of the growing interest in Chinese language programs across Ohio. Since its initiation in 2006, the OSU K-12 Chinese Flagship Program has made significant contributions to Ohio schools and teachers, including the following support and services:

- Two statewide conferences for school administrators on how to start and maintain successful Chinese language programs (each time attracting about 200 in December);
- Site visits to most of the 50 schools/districts currently offering Chinese with technical assistance provided to administrators;
- Class observation of most of the current 57 Chinese language teachers with recommendations provided to teachers;
- Development of the first phase of K-1 curriculum kit, which will be piloted at Gahanna-Jefferson Public Schools and possibly other schools;
- Completion of a first level textbook, *Chinese: Communicating in the Culture,* with a MP3 audio program and an interactive DVD.
- Development of lesson plans and teacher's guide for 9-10th graders based on *Chinese: Communicating in the Culture* and other instructional material;
- Four one-day professional development workshops for Chinese language teachers at no cost to teachers or schools;
- Creating the Ohio Association of Teachers of Chinese (OATC), with 28 paid members;
- Obtaining StarTalk funds to operate Chinese Immersion Summer Day Camps during June 16-27 in three metro areas of Cleveland, Columbus, and Dayton;
- Resources to schools, teachers and other citizens through daily communications and website (http://k12chineseflagship.osu.edu);
- Building a pilot global classroom at Metro High School that can be connected with other classrooms in Ohio and in China;
- Facilitating a partnership between the Columbus Metro High School and Ohio Contemporary Chinese School; and
- Developing a corporate partnership brochure and making initial contacts to help create a pipeline of Chinese speaking professionals in Ohio.

As the demand increases, we plan on increasing support to schools and teachers. While we continue to support more schools starting Chinese language programs in the future, we want to focus on helping the existing programs to increase quality and expand their offerings. Some of our tasks in the next twelve months would include:

- Accelerating the development of K-12 curricula;
- Intensifying professional development for current teachers;
- Supporting the activities of the newly formed Ohio Association of Teachers of Chinese;

- Increasing the number and quality of partner schools so they can become models for others;
- Facilitating partnerships between all partner schools with local heritage schools;
- Helping more partner schools to build global classrooms;
- Strengthening our statewide efforts in promoting Chinese language through coordinated projects (e.g., StarTalk funded Summer Day Camps);
- Providing more web-based resources for teachers and administrators;
- Better planning for program development by visiting all schools with Chinese programs and observing classes of all teachers; and
- Developing corporate partnerships to generate mutually beneficial support.

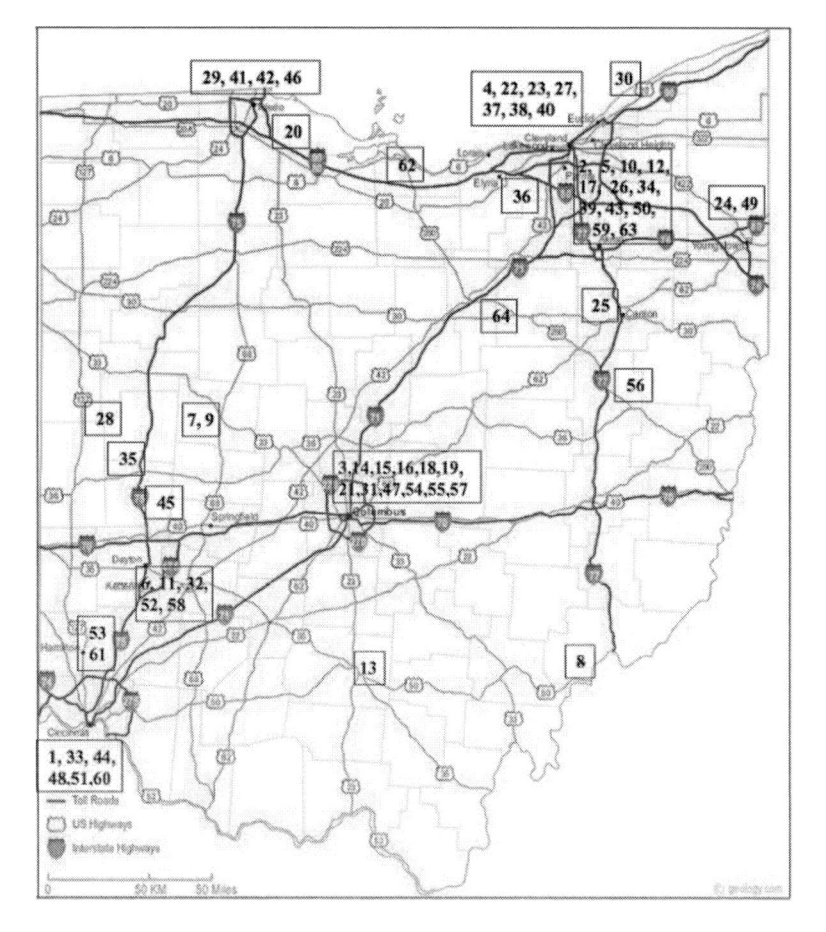

Distribution of Ohio Schools and Districts with Chinese Language Programs (Numbers correspond to schools listed on the following pages).

Ohio represents "the heart of America" in many ways. If the multifaceted partnership model in providing Chinese language and culture works for K-12 schools in Ohio, it should work for schools in many other states. The OSU K-12 Chinese Flagship Program is determined to work with all its partners to help Ohio schools succeed in mainstreaming Chinese language in K-12 schools.

For more information about K-12 Chinese in Ohio and the OSU K-12 Chinese Flagship Program, please visit http://k12chineseflagship.osu.edu.

**Ohio Schools and Districts with Chinese Programs in 2007–08 (matching the numbers marked on the map above; private schools with *)**

| # | School/District | School Webpage |
|---|---|---|
| 1 | Academy of World Languages (Cincinnati) | http://awl.cps-k12.org |
| 2 | Akron City Schools | http://www.akron.k12.oh.us/dept/014 |
| 3 | Arts and College Prep. Academy (Columbus) | www.artcollegeprep.com |
| 4 | Avon Local Schools | www.avon.k12.oh.us |
| 5 | Beachwood City Schools | www.beachwood.k12.oh.us |
| 6 | Beavercreek City Schools | www.beavercreek.k12.oh.us |
| 7 | Bellefontaine City Schools | http://www.bellefontaine.k12.oh.us |
| 8 | Belpre City Schools (cancelled for 2008-09) | www.belpre.k12.oh.us |
| 9 | Benjamin Logan Local Schools | http://www.benlogan.k12.oh.us |
| 10 | Brecksville-Broadview Heights City Schools | http://www.bbhcsd.k12.oh.us |
| 11 | Centerville High School | http://www.centerville.k12.oh.us |
| 12 | Chagrin Falls EV Schools - HS | http://www.chagrin-falls.k12.oh.us |
| 13 | Chillicothe City Schools | http://www.chillicothe.k12.oh.us |
| 14 | Columbus Academy * | http://www.columbusacademy.org |
| 15 | Columbus Alternative High School | http://www.cahs.info |
| 16 | Columbus School for Girls * | http://www.columbusschoolforgirls.org |
| 17 | Crestwood Local Schools | http://crestwood.sparcc.org |
| 18 | Diocese of Columbus – Catholic Schools * | http://www.cdeducation.org/doe |
| 19 | Gahanna-Jefferson Public Schools | http://www.gahannaschools.org |
| 20 | Genoa Area Local Schools | http://www.genoa.k12.oh.us |
| 21 | Groveport Madison High School | http://www.gocruisers.org |
| 22 | Hathaway Brown School (Shaker Heights) * | http://www.hb.edu |
| 23 | Hawken School (Cleveland) * | http://www.hawken.edu |
| 24 | Hubbard Exempted Village Schools | http://www.hubbard.k12.oh.us |
| 25 | Jackson Local Schools (Massillon) | http://jackson.stark.k12.oh.us |
| 26 | Kent City Schools | http://www.kent.k12.oh.us |
| 27 | Laurel School (Shaker Heights) * | http://www.laurelschool.org |
| 28 | Marion Local School District (Mercer Co.) | http://marionlocal.k12.oh.us |
| 29 | Maumee Valley Country Day School (Toledo)* | http://www.mvcds.org |
| 30 | Mentor Public Schools | http://www.mentorschools.org |
| 31 | Metro High School (Columbus) | www.themetroschool.com |
| 32 | Miami Valley School (Dayton) * | http://www.mvschool.com |
| 33 | Nativity School (Cincinnati) * | http://www.nativity-cincinnati.org |
| 34 | Parma City Schools | http://www.parmacityschools.org |
| 35 | Piqua City Schools | http://portal.piqua.org |
| 36 | Polaris Career Center | http://www.polaris.edu |
| 37 | Saint Joseph Academy (Cleveland) * | http://www.sja1890.org |

**(Continued)**

| # | School/District | School Webpage |
|---|---|---|
| 38 | Shaker Heights City Schools | http://www.shaker.org |
| 39 | Solon City Schools – Solon High School | http://www.solonschools.org/shs |
| 40 | South Euclid - Lyndhurst City Schools | http://www.sel.k12.oh.us |
| 41 | Springfield Local Schools (Lucas Co.) | http://springfield-lucas.us |
| 42 | St. John's Jesuit Academy (Toledo) * | http://www.sjjtitans.org |
| 43 | Summit Academy Schools (community schools; Copley) | http://www.summitacademies.com/default2.htm |
| 44 | Summit Country Day School (Cincinnati) * | www.summitcds.org |
| 45 | Tipp City Exempted Village Schools | http://www.tippcityschools.com |
| 46 | Toledo Public Schools – Start High School | http://www.tps.org |
| 47 | Village Academy Schools (Powell) * | www.villageacademyschools.org |
| 48 | VLT Academy (community; Cincinnati) | http://www.swoca.net/about/dist/VLTA.html |
| 49 | Warren Harding High School | http://www.warrenschools.k12.oh.us |
| 50 | Western Reserve Academy (Hudson) * | http://www.wra.net |
| 51 | Winton Woods City Schools | http://www.wintonwoods.org |
| | **New Schools and Districts with Chinese Programs in 2008–09** **(Matching the numbers marked on the map above)** | |
| 52 | Bellbrook High School | http://www.sugarcreek.k12.oh.us |
| 53 | Butler Tech. and Career Development Schools | http://www.butlertech.org |
| 54 | Canal Winchester Local Schools | http://www.canalwin.k12.oh.us |
| 55 | Columbus Public Schools | http://www.columbus.k12.oh.us |
| 56 | Dover High School | http://www.dover.k12.oh.us |
| 57 | Dublin City Schools | http://www.dublinschools.net |
| 58 | Fairborn High School (Dayton) | http://www.fairborn.k12.oh.us |
| 59 | Kenston Local Schools (Chagrin Falls) | http://www.kenston.k12.oh.us |
| 60 | Loveland City Schools | http://www.lovelandschools.org |
| 61 | Mason City School District | http://www.masonohioschools.com |
| 62 | Ottawa Hills Local Schools | http://www.ohschools.k12.oh.us |
| 63 | Rootstown Local Schools | http://sparcc.rootstown.com |
| 64 | Wooster City Schools | http://www.wooster.k12.oh.us |

(Note: Nativity School began offering Chinese in April 2008.)

(Note: More schools or districts may start Chinese language programs in 2008-09.)

# QINGDAO FLAGSHIP CENTER

Qingdao is a city of the future in China: it has been declared one of five cities to receive special investment from China's central government for the current Five Year Plan, it is one of the few designated "green" cities in China, it was the site of the 2008 Olympic outdoor water sports, and it has recently been voted the city most Chinese would like to move to in a recent national poll. Qingdao is a city on the cutting edge of China's rising economy and at the same time provides an environment that persons from other places in the world will find interesting and comfortable, whether they are China specialists or not. Qingdao is quickly developing as an international city that is attracting people from all over the world and is a good host to young Americans seeking opportunities to participate in the life of the community. For these reasons, we have chosen Qingdao as the operational center for our activities in China. These include summer programs, internship placement and management, and student research and community service projects, and program and materials development.

**Summer Programs:** During the summer the Qingdao Flagship Center manages instructional programs designed to raise student proficiency levels to advanced threshold, advanced, and superior threshold. While the first two programs are both designed for training learners whose Chinese skills are near or at ILR Level 2, they differ mainly in their focuses and the corresponding pedagogical approaches. Advanced threshold courses are for students needing systematic training in basic language areas in order to perform effectively, and its curriculum provides a more structured classroom instruction plus measured amount of social practicum experience. The Advanced level program is for those who are prepared to engage with a Chinese community and to communicate ideas with native Chinese speakers in authentic and non-textbook contexts. Its curriculum is theme-based and task-motivated and its instruction is more dynamic and requires a much larger amount of social practicum. The superior threshold program prepares those who are in China for their final Flagship year. To assure they can function as independent learners, researchers, and interns before they begin their career as cross-cultural and bilingual professionals, we put them through a curriculum that provides intensive and individualized one-on-one mentoring focusing on refining the exchange of ideas (through oral discussion and essay writing) in the register of working professionals, undertaking individualized community service projects, and performing-in-context projects aimed at preparing the students engage and establish themselves in a Chinese community.

The Qingdao Flagship Center is responsible for the design and execution of the curriculums for these programs, design and directing all social practicum projects, and managing local logistical means to secure the realization of these projects by coordinating with various Flagship programs from different US institutions, recruitment, training and management of local instructors, mentors and learning partners, negotiation with local hosting institutions for local onsite support, and monitoring and directing the progress of the students.

As the number of undergraduate students increase and as the undergraduate Flagship programs develop, the Center is also expected to work with different Chinese educational institutions and corporations to develop a flexible range of courses and community- practicum opportunities to accommodate students with a variety of backgrounds in Chinese language and culture—first timers, repeatvisitors, and learners who "picked up" their Chinese language through a variety of means other than the typical American undergraduate foreign language program.

As the K-12 Flagship program develops, the Qingdao Center will assume the task of working with the K-12 Flagship program in identifying and negotiating appropriate sites and partners for various types of in-China programs for high school students. It will also be working on developing courses and preparing activities that are appropriate for these students and ensure they have linguistically productive experiences through these programs.

**Internship Placement and Management:** One of the most important and most challenging tasks for the Qingdao Flagship Center is internship placement and management.

The internship is the means by which Flagship students demonstrate the real world knowledge and skills that verify their qualifications as cross-cultural and bi-lingual professionals to themselves and to our program. Internships are typically served in Chinese organizations that are chosen to reflect each student's domain and where a single Flagship student joins a Chinese workforce. Their bosses are Chinese managers and their colleagues expect them to contribute to the goals of the organization. It is from the internship experience that students report the greatest gain in ability to achieve their intentions in Chinese. It is also from the internship experience that our program gains the most valuable feedback, where we discover what programmatic elements have effectively contributed to our students' success and which have not. The internship is key to our program consistently producing Americans with truly advanced skills in Chinese language and culture.

The management of this internship program is challenging because of the great variety of domains and career interests the of the Flagship students. Much time is spent in identifying appropriate internship sites and persuading the organizations to host a Flagship student. We insist that each host organization invest resources in the internship, providing housing or living stipend—or both from the more affluent enterprises. We have found that an investment on their part raises the expectations of the intern contributing to their organization and these heightened expectations raise the standard for the whole experience. For most Chinese organizations, the concept and practice of internships are still a novelty. Thus, it requires extensive negotiations with potential internship hosts and intensive training of our students to develop strategies by which they can quickly become genuine contributors to the host organization. The Qingdao Flagship Center first works with each student to identify the type of internship that is most fitting for the student's study, research plan and career interest. It then utilizes its resources and connections to identify possible internship sites and to negotiate with the potential internship hosts. Inevitably, some adjustments have to be made by one or both sides, and the Center keeps in very close communications with both sides in this process. While student preferences and internship host desires will be carefully considered, the Center has the responsibility to also take into consideration the Flagship mission and makes the final decision on what will be the most suitable internship program for any given student. Since we have now interns throughout the year (fall, spring and summer) and all over China, and since we will place no more than one Flagship intern into one internship site, this process will always be an on-going one.

Before the internship starts, the Center runs a "Pre-internship Workshop" for all Flagship interns. Through site visits, lectures and discussions led by working professionals in related fields, and a series of hands-on training sessions, the workshop focuses on furthering the knowledge and practice of the types of behavioral culture having a direct impact on how one establishes oneself in a Chinese working place and the skills necessary for navigating effectively and productively in such environments.

During the internship, the Center continues to work with both the interns and the internship hosts to ensure the internship will be executed in an optimal way. Since the great majority of the Chinese internship hosts still do not treat internship very seriously and thus do not have specific internship procedures, the Center needs, on the one hand, continuously to work with internship hosts to further develop their internship programs for the Flagship interns, and, on the other hand, work with the students to develop knowledge of and skills for being accepted into a Chinese organization and being treated as a capable professional. After the internship the Center continues to work with the internship hosts on matters such as feedback on the Flagship interns' performances, maintaining relationships, and developing a network of potential internship sites for the growing Flagship internship needs.

The success of our internships is reflected in the repeated requests from host organizations for additional and continuous Flagship students and by the frequent times the host organization seeks to continue a relationship with a student after the internship is completed.

**Student Research and Thesis Projects:** Integrating research projects into a student's study and internship experience in China ensures that the time spent there is meaningful and productive. To different degrees, most Flagship students in China have research assignments from their respective home institutions while each of the OSU Flagship students is expected to conduct research at a level that will be useful for their master's thesis projects. Before the student comes to China, the Qingdao Flagship Center director works closely with the student and his/her academic advisor in the home institution in drafting a China research plan that is meaningful and doable. When the student is in China, the center director continues to provide advice to the student on fine tuning his/her research plan, identifying places and means, and developing strategies to carry out the plan. Typically, the Center will work the student's research plan into his/her internship program, arrange local mentors who are experts in the field the student is working on, monitor the progress of the research, make all necessary adjustments including adjustments to the student's research plan and adjustments to his/her internship program and study program, arrange local editorial assistance, and identify and arrange Chinese experts to participate in the student's thesis defense through video conferencing from Center.

**Program Development:** In addition to the summer study programs and the year round internship programs, the Qingdao Center is also working on developing a series of programs that will be mutually beneficial to the Flagship mission, OSU programs, and American education in general:

*Global Classroom Programs:* Through video conferencing, we have developed several educational and cultural events with a cross cultural and bilingual context, such as internship conference between Flagship interns currently conducting internship in China and Flagship students currently studying in their US home institutions; thesis defenses participated in by students, American professors and Chinese experts in related domains; and "cultural salon" events dealing with misconceptions between China and the US, traditional folk art in contemporary China, and educational issues in the US and China. Discussions are underway about developing courses that will bring together learners and experts from both China and the US and thus create a global learning context dealing with topics such as Professional Networking in China and the US, Conflicting Viewpoints, Perspectives and Presentations on Chinese Civilization, Comparative Studies of Chinese and American Behavioral Culture, and American Studies Courses in Chinese Universities.

*Teacher Training Programs:* Training in foreign language pedagogy theories, approaches, and techniques for both Chinese teachers teaching Chinese to foreign learners and Chinese teachers teaching English to Chinese learners. Both the field of teaching Chinese to foreign learners and the field of teaching English to Chinese learners are expanding rapidly in China and the bottle-neck for the healthy development of these fields is the severe lack of teachers trained in effective instruction. The Center will work with both the local universities (Qingdao University, China Ocean University) to create foreign language teacher training programs for local teachers and some leading national universities (Tsinghua University, Beijing University, Jinan University, Wuhan University) to create Qingdao based national foreign language teacher training programs. Creating a cadre of effective teachers in China will have an important impact on American programs.

**Material Development:** Utilizing the relatively easy access to authentic contemporary Chinese materials and native Chinese speaker resources, the Center will engage in the development of a series of instructional materials for the Flagship program. These materials will be developed in audio, video, DVD and other types of digital formats (both online and off line), and printed textbooks. Currently a material development team headed by the center director and assisted by the local staff is being assembled to plan the following projects:

*Professional Networking in China and the US*: this course has taught in the OSU US-China Links program and Flagship program for many years and it is one of the most fundamental and effective courses in our program. We have accumulated a rich collection of materials and experience that can be brought a useful set of materials.

*Viewpoints, Perspectives and Presentations on US-China Relations*: this is one of the hottest and most easily mishandled issues between the two countries. The course and its instructional material will focus on familiarizing the students with Chinese perspectives, their ways of presenting those perspectives and effective strategies for responding to these viewpoints.

*Classical Chinese in Contemporary Chinese discourse*: The focus of this course and its materials is not to teach classical Chinese as such, but to familiarize students with a body of Chinese classical texts that is still very much present in modern Mandarin. The goal of these materials is to train the students to comprehend these texts and use them appropriately and effectively in the context of contemporary Chinese discourse. Command of this kind of language is taken as a mark of how sophisticated one's comprehension of Chinese culture is as well as how serious one's commitment to learning the Chinese language is. Consequently, it has direct impact on if one will be perceived as a serious participant in the discourse of Chinese professionals.

## OHIO LANGUAGE SUMMIT AND THE
## *OHIO LANGUAGE ROADMAP FOR THE 21ST CENTURY*

## I. Introduction

On June 28, 2007 the Ohio Language Summit was held in Columbus at the Center for Science and Industry (COSI), sponsored locally by the OSU Chinese Flagship Program, the Educational Council, and the Ohio Department of Development and nationally by the US Departments of Defense, Commerce, and Labor. From across Ohio, eighty-five participants from business, government, public service, and academics met to discuss the relationship between foreign language and culture knowledge and the future of our State. The business and government participants (65%) represented the **demand** for people with language and culture skills and the educators (35%) represented those who can affect the **supply** of these people in Ohio. Together they identified and prioritized the critical domestic and international language needs in Ohio. This was followed by a series of meetings of two Roadmap Design Teams--one domestic and one international--who prepared a report based on the findings of the Language Summit and their subsequent deliberations. On October 25, 2007, a condensed version of this report, titled *Ohio Language Roadmap for the 21st Century (http:// chineseflagship.osu.edu/ohiolanguagesummit/LanguageSummitReport.pdf)*, was presented at an event where Dr. David S.C. Chu, United States Under Secretary of Defense; Lt. Governor Lee Fisher, director of the Ohio Department of Development; Dr. Joseph Alutto, Provost of Ohio State University; Deborah Gavlik, Associate Vice Chancellor, Board of Regents, Dr. Susan Zelman, Ohio Superintendent of Public Instruction; and Professor Galal Walker, addressed the content of the document and it relevance to the economic and political security of our State and Nation.

The process continues: this event has been followed with subsequent meetings of the Design Teams who have further elaborated the descriptions and strategized the implementation of the five recommendations of the *Roadmap*, namely the 1) establishment of a Language and Culture Service Center, 2) a citizens' advocacy group, 3) extended sequences of language instruction in Ohio schools, 4) extensive teacher training that includes the capacity to employ technology, and 5) performance assessments in the crucial languages. Subsequently under the leadership of Dr. Randy Smith, Vice-Provost for Academic Affairs, Ohio State has convened representatives of 13 public universities in Ohio to discuss sharing resources to create the Language and Culture Service Center, extended sequences of language instruction, and the citizens' advocacy group. In addition, Ohio State is exploring the creation of an Institute of Advanced Language Study devoted to producing global professionals in a number of languages. The goal of these meetings among the public universities of Ohio is to present a multi-institutional proposal to the newly formed University System of Ohio to establish joint efforts to deal with these issues of language and culture education. This activity is in line with the Strategic Plan for the University System of Ohio (http://uso.edu/ strategicplan/handbook/uso/relationships.php#50) recently promulgated by its Chancellor Eric Fingerhut. Influenced by recent activities of the Ohio Department of Education, the *Ohio Language Roadmap for the 21st Century,* consulting with Dr. Robert Slater, and the realization that global education has a direct relevance to Ohio's future, the Strategic Plan includes these actions aimed at strengthening international education:

- The University System of Ohio will encourage foreign language learning and will promote the teaching of less commonly taught languages critical to support the state's international trade linkages (such as the languages of Ohio's top 20 trade partners) and the country's national security interests.
- The University System of Ohio and the Partnership for Continued Learning will work with the K-12 system to encourage the study of foreign languages as early as possible.

- The University System of Ohio will work with Ohio's private colleges and universities to develop shared programs for study abroad that are more affordable to Ohio students.
- The University System of Ohio will work with Ohio's private institutions and the Ohio Department of Development to jointly market and promote Ohio's higher education offerings across the globe and to share the costs of recruiting international students.
- The Board of Regents will encourage Ohio institutions to measure the satisfaction of international students with the services provided at Ohio campuses and to compare them to key competitors in the United States and abroad in order to improve services.
- The Board of Regents will work with the Ohio Department of Development to identify Ohio companies that have a significant global presence to develop internship opportunities for Ohio students, provide these businesses with higher education resources to support their work in other countries, and to help solve overseas shortages of skilled manpower through sponsored training and recruitment of foreign nationals to Ohio's institutions.
- The Board of Regents will collect, through the Higher Education Information system, international educational data concerning students, scholars, international educational opportunities, and research activities.

We found that agencies in government and public service have critical, sometimes life-and-death, needs for language and culture expertise and that businesses have the same needs in order to grow their markets. In Ohio, business participation did not primarily come from the major corporations that are already engaged in large-scale international trade. Rather representatives of small and medium sized firms who see international involvement as part of their growth pattern were much more interested in contributing to this effort. As it turns out, it is these kinds of firms that are driving economic development in Ohio. Our Lt. Governor has stated:

> Entrepreneurship is a key factor in turning Ohio's economy around. In many respects, Ohio's future economic prosperity will be built around new ideas, new products and new processes that capitalize on our state's existing assets and leverage global opportunities. That's why Ohio is dedicated to helping early-stage businesses by expanding access to capital, thus improving the commercial viability of their generation of products and services. (see *Poised for Growth: 2007 Ohio Venture Capital Report,* Fisher College of Business, Center for Entrepreneurship)

This level of business involvement is consistent with combining language with culture and technical knowledge with an eye toward economic development—a reoccurring theme in the deliberations of the Roadmap Design Teams.

One of the discoveries of the Language Summit and Roadmap activities is the realization that our communities include numerous talented people who have rich experiences in dealing with other cultures and languages that they are willing to share with their fellow citizens. These global citizens are our best resource for building the capacity to meet the challenges a global century will bring to our State and Nation.

The following account reflects the on-going concerns and deliberations of the Ohioans who are participating in these activities. We conclude this section with appendices presenting some of the data the Design Teams considered in their deliberations.

*Critical Domestic Language Needs*

1) *What are the languages in which Ohio needs improved capacity?*
   Spanish, Chinese, Somali, Russian, Japanese, Korean, Arabic, French, Amharic, Fulani

2) *What are the areas in which foreign language/cultural skill are needed?*
   External: customer service; identifying and developing markets; medical/legal services; developing and presenting financial products; government and social services to immigrant/migrant communities (such as family services, economic aid, worker safety training); libraries Internal: manager-employee relations; finding qualified language instructors

3) *What are costs associated with lack of foreign language skills?*
   Shortage of qualified teachers; lost business with Muslim community (e.g., financial products); monolingual companies lose immigrant community's business to firms that can reach out to them; poor medical/emergency interpretation is life-threatening; time spent on cross-cultural issues in organizations with significant number of foreign-born employees; corporate image problem; lawsuits over non-performance of Title VI requirements; inability to measure level of skills of interpreters/translators; cost of outsourcing foreign language skills to third-party vendors

4) *What are the current solutions or "work-arounds" to situations requiring language and culture skills?*
   Hire bilingual employees to reach out to immigrant communities; outsource translation/interpretation to outside vendors; hire English-speaking foreign nationals as interpreters or in-house bridges; utilize family members (children) to interpret for non-English-speaking elders, provide diversity training; create multilingual websites; develop PR campaigns for information dissemination, ignore opportunities that require language and culture capacity.

*Critical International Language Needs*

1) *What languages are needed?*
   Arabic, Chinese, Hindi, Spanish, Japanese, Portuguese, Russian, Vietnamese, French, Korean, German, Somali, Hebrew, Italian, Hindi

2) *Where are foreign language and cultural skills needed?*
   Marketing to foreign nationals/firms, especially in the auto industry and agriculture; understanding foreign regulations, especially regarding medical devices; engaging in negotiation, especially in the intermediate levels of corporate contacts abroad; contract translation; customer service.

3) *What costs are associated with lack of foreign language skills?*
Lost contracts; bad national and corporate image; serious inaccuracies due to the lack of a match between the technical knowledge and language knowledge on the part of translators/interpreters; good ideas opportunities often lost in - or due to lack of – translation (reduces the talent pool in global organization to English-speakers); loss of competitiveness in global markets.

5) *What are the current solutions or "work-arounds" to situations requiring language and culture skills?*
Hire interpreters, provide training/education to increase Americans' foreign language/cultural skills; use language/cultural skills of heritage speakers, take persons off their regular job assignments to deal with language issues, avoid markets or sources that require language skills.

## Questions from the Supply-Side (Public and Private Language Educators) to the Demand-Side:

- How much language education is "enough" and what should the content include?
- How can supply and demand side organizations partner to produce what the demand-side needs?
- What language/cultural skills are needed and used in business?

| Demand priorities | Critical Ohio Language Themes | Supply priorities |
|---|---|---|
| 1 | The need for a workforce that is highly skilled in content expertise and language proficiency | 4 |
| 2 | Cultural sensitivity and knowledge, plus language skills are needed for customer retention and market expansion | |
| 3 | Need to provide meaningful incentives development of language and cultural capacity for | 6 |
| 4 | The need for language and cultural skills across The spectrum of proficiency levels, from Basic to Superior | 1 |
| 5 | A need for a global change in the way Americans regard the importance of language learning and culture skills | 2 |
| Two tied for 6th place | * Quality Control Issues: There is a need for accurate field-specific translations and interpretations. <br> * A public education campaign to educate The community in the value of being culturally competent and having language skills. | 5 |
| | Need linguistic and cultural awareness training to create a welcoming destination for foreign direct investment in Ohio | 3 |
| | * Acute need for Somali (in central Ohio) and Spanish language training for medical/safety/emergency services <br> * Train interpreters to understand the culture of The people with whom they are working | Two tied for 7th position |

## Critical Ohio Language Themes

Language Summit Supply and Demand participants identified 12 themes relevant to Ohio's language needs. Each group then determined the six most critical language needs in Ohio as listed below.

Following this meeting, we invited two teams of concerned and uniquely qualified Ohioans to address the international and domestic challenges facing the State in its determination to expand its economy, improve its foreign language education, and deepen the understanding of its place in the world on the part of its citizenry. These are the bases for assuring the future security of the State and the Nation and are what we intend to address in *Ohio Language Roadmap for the 21st Century*. The members of these teams believe that globalization of the world economy is on-going and members of the teams observe that national economies in some parts of the world are expanding explosively. If Ohio is to thrive in this global competition, we will need management and a workforce that can interact creatively and effectively with people from other cultures, be able to glean information and innovations wherever they may occur in the world, capitalize on Ohio's strategic location, resources, and capabilities, and fully develop opportunities where the state has a sustainable competitive advantage. Some Design Team members see the failure to act decisively in preparing the Ohio economy to participate fully in the global arena as a major failure of foresight and will. Consequently, Ohio must invest in preparing our people and organizations to deal with linguistic and cultural complexity by creating programs and institutions to promote and develop a broad capacity to conduct business effectively in the 21st century.

The Language Summit and the subsequent final report, the *Ohio Language Roadmap for the 21st Century,* are essentially a citizens' effort to identify is educational issues in the global challenges facing Ohio and possible solutions to resolve our shortcomings. The purpose here is to state the basic situation and then challenge ourselves and others, especially those in leadership roles, to step up and lay the foundations for a better response to what looks like an inevitable future.

## II. Strategic Vision

We see Ohio gaining a strategic advantage by redefining the role foreign language ability plays in Americans' educational and professional lives. Solidifying Ohio's successes in foreign trade and attracting foreign labor requires recognizing the importance of foreign language skills in building trusting relationships with non-native speakers of English at home and abroad. From the national to the local level, trust between communities from different cultures reduces the potential for conflict, increases the opportunities for cooperation, and advances collective security. The Roadmap Design Teams' action recommendations for Ohioans in government, business and education are captured by one strategic vision:

**In Ohio, businesses, government agencies, and educational institutions will collaborate to create a multilingual workforce by developing innovative programs that assure Ohioans of opportunities to gain advanced knowledge of foreign languages and cultures in conjunction with job-related technical and academic knowledge.**

Building a strong multi-lingual workforce that opens untapped global and domestic markets creates a stronger Ohio economy. Our vision is that Ohioans with professionally-useful foreign language ability will create positive, trusting relationships with people of other cultures and that these relationships will lead to the creation of new jobs and businesses. By leading the nation in strengthening global economic ties, Ohioans will also lead the nation in strengthening state and national security through their ability to communicate effectively in critical languages.

These global professionals able to establish trusting relationships with speakers of foreign languages will be the product of innovative educational resources that promote lifelong culture and language learning from elementary school into the workplace. Ohio can lead the nation by developing a visionary approach to early language and culture study that combines language study with core educational content such as mathematics, science, and social studies. In this way Ohio students can become global professionals, able to communicate with counterparts around the world on occupational and academic topics. This approach works not only with English speakers learning other languages, but also in helping Ohio's new immigrants become proficient in communicating their expertise in dual language environments. Through distance learning technology, this model can be promoted in the work place.

As a nation of immigrants, the United States is in a unique position to be the cross-language, cross-cultural broker of world trade and finance. If Ohio can recognize this potential and act on it, adding language ability to our marketing and management skills will keep Ohio competitive in a global service economy.

## III. Action Agenda

Strategic visions become reality through actions. To realize the strategic vision, the Ohio Design Teams divided their action recommendations into a set of projects to promote the supply of foreign language instruction and learning and a set of projects to increase the demand for foreign language skills. Some of the recommendations require dramatic decision-making by Ohio's political, business and education leadership. Some would be low or no cost changes in the way organizations regard language and culture issues in our state.

### *A. Pulling Together Resources to Implement the Roadmap*

### Action Item 1: Establish an Ohio Language and Culture Service Center (LCSC)

The Design Teams focused on the concept of a service center that would develop and organize foreign language and culture expertise. This expertise would be devoted to assisting Ohio citizens and organizations deal with the themes that emerged from the Language Summit. This Ohio LCSC could be located in an appropriate government agency, in an institution of higher learning, or even exist as an independent non-profit organization, but it would be tasked with providing the basic infrastructure for expanding and improving the learning of foreign languages and cultures in the state and the application of language and culture skills in Ohio's public and private sectors. This center could also have satellite locations throughout the state (libraries, education centers, heritage community centers), connected by technologies and shared interests.

The Roadmap Design Teams propose that the basic functions of such an organization include:

1) Developing and managing databases of individuals available to Ohioans who have certified language proficiency combined with expertise in technical and occupational areas, public and private resources for dealing with language and culture needs, and employment opportunities requiring language and culture skills

2) Organizing and managing projects requiring foreign language capabilities (e.g., developing foreign language web sites for companies and government agencies, researching markets in other countries, public relations campaigns in foreign languages)

3) Consulting and advising on educational programs in foreign languages, including providing summer language field study and study abroad opportunities for Ohiolanguage students and teachers. The LCSC should function as a clearinghouse for language and culture learning opportunities for all Ohioans seeking to expand their abilities to successfully navigate other societies.

4) Organizing teacher training and advising on the development of foreign language programs

5) Providing assessment of students' and professionals' foreign language skills and foreign language programs

1) Serving as a venue for the interface between government offices and constituents where language issues arise.

*What are the outcomes of such a center?*

The LCSC would be one location where Ohioans and Ohio companies could go to when confronting a problem involving language. If the Ohio LCSC is unable to provide a solution, it should be able to identify available resources, give examples of previous solutions developed for similar problems, estimate the cost of a solution and be prepared to organize and manage projects. The LCSC would provide the means by which qualified individuals can find cross-cultural work and where Ohioans can improve their knowledge of foreign cultures and languages through access to resources such as Ohio State's Individualized Instruction and on-line courses taught by colleges and universities across the state.

The LCSC will have updated information on services such as language hotlines where law enforcement, courts, hospitals or security stations at airports can call to find the appropriate interpretation service. If care is taken when planning and organizing the LCSC, it will also be a "go to" organization where immigrants feel comfortable. As such it will be an ideal venue for government representatives to reach out to immigrant communities to inform them about government policies and programs.

The end goal of establishing the LCSC is to aggregate and nurture the resources necessary for transitioning Ohio from a manufacturing-based economy strongly affected by off-shoring of operations to a robust future-oriented economy drawing strength and resilience from Ohio's strategic location, resources, and capabilities, and from dynamic expansion into national and global markets where the state has a sustainable competitive advantage.

To be successful the LCSC would have to be built on a broad collaboration of education, government, and business. The expertise of our strongest educational institutions must accommodate the needs of government agencies and businesses, share information on personnel and resources, and a provider-client relationship nurtured. If we are right in predicting that Ohio's economy will become increasingly global, the demand for these services will be sufficient to sustain the expert staff this facility will require.

*Which organizations might be the drivers for this project?*

Three state agencies are most concerned with cross-cultural interaction: the Ohio Departments of Development, Agriculture and Jobs and Family Services. The Departments of Development and Agriculture are tasked with creating job opportunities for Ohioans through export and foreign direct investment; the department of Jobs and Family Services is responsible for making sure that available job opportunities and government services are communicated to all Ohioans, including those with limited English proficiency. Federal agencies in Labor, Commerce, Education and Health & Human Services will be interested in the LCSC because of the positive impact on workforce and trade. Trade associations will find added capacity for their membership to engage foreign language communities. Law enforcement agencies such as the TSA, FBI, and local police will appreciate having a one-stop location for resolving language issues. The Ohio Department of Education will have a powerful resource for implementing its future foreign language policies.

*What would be the timeframe for establishing such an organization?*

The LCSC will require five years to establish funding, staff and a physical location. If an existing facility such as the World Media and Culture Center at Ohio State could be expanded to serve this function, the timeframe might be shortened. The first two years need to be devoted to developing and managing standardized assessments, assessing foreign language speakers and building the databases that will serve as the basis for Ohio LCSC consulting operations.

*How the Ohio LCSC Contributes to the Strategic Vision*

Such a Center will serve both a symbolic and practical function. It will symbolize to Ohio the social value of individuals from other countries and of Ohioans who have developed the capacity to effectively communicate in foreign languages and cultures. Through the use of a variety of world media technology such as satellite television and Internet news sources with electronic dictionaries, the Center and its affiliated locations around the state can embody the spirit of the strategic vision, providing a venue for continued learning of language and culture as well as developing a welcoming social environment where heritage communities and their Ohio neighbors can interact.

The mutual understanding that comes from interaction and education reduces the mistrust that exists between cultures; the concentration of foreign language and culture expertise and language-related activities produces an environment here in Ohio where any American can be immersed in the foreign culture of their study or interest.

## Action Item 2: Create a Networking Organization, Language Partnering for Life (LPL)

Roadmap Design Teams suggest that the LCSC organize a service organization that brings together public and private groups with a stake in cross-cultural understanding and communication. This group, tentatively named Language Partnering for Life (LPL), will be associated with the Ohio LCSC and will provide the community base for life-long learning, putting individuals in touch with native speakers of languages they are studying and activities based on the media sources of the Center. Functioning like a Rotary Club with many language-based sub-groups, the LPL will organize international events, culture-festivals, trips abroad, and study groups. Drawing on the leadership of business and public organizations with vested interests in cross-cultural communication, the LPL will provide the social motivation for continued language learning and for networking with persons of like interests.

Functioning in conjunction with the Ohio LCSC, this organization can provide the state agencies, local governments, and Ohio businesses with access to individuals who can facilitate interactions with foreign visitors who are in Ohio to conduct business or simply to enjoy the amenities of the state. The LPL could play a key role in making sure foreign tourists and sojourners in Ohio have a good chance to experience the state on a personal level by including them in LPL activities and introducing them to LPL members across the state. Working with the LCSC, LPL will develop language and culture training programs for organizations and localities interested in attracting foreign direct investment to Ohio. Ohio has much to offer foreign firms, but it must be packaged and presented in such a way that these firms are made to feel welcome to Ohio.

Using the facilities of the LCSC and LPL, or the affiliated language programs of universities, colleges and community colleges, individualized instruction programs, specialized language study groups (e.g., "business Spanish"), or language maintenance courses such as Japanese-for-anime-fans can be offered as a volunteer or fee-based activity. University language programs can cooperate to create foreign language mentorships such as Engineering in French or Medical Care in Somali. These venues can be made accessible to a wide range of learners and can involve members of heritage communities and special interest groups who want to share their languages and cultures.

*What are the desired outcomes of the LPL?*

The LPL office will compile a list of interested stakeholders in Ohio's globally-oriented communities and be the driving force behind information sharing and networking among them. This information sharing will help guide funding to groups who need it, help groups find synergies for growth, and help organizations with similar goals pool their resources. One example of such organizations are Ohio's sister city associations. Ohio cities with sister cities abroad currently act independently of each other, and, for the most part[1] , independently of other organizations in their city such as local universities, law enforcement, chambers of commerce, and even local government offices. Through personal connections in the LPL, Ohio cities and their sisters abroad will discover rich opportunities for cross-cultural learning and trade.[2]

The LPL office will also organize meetings of its members so that the demand side of the world language equation can regularly communicate their needs to the supply side. With regular input from the end users of the education system's product, educators can continuously improve foreign language education to fit current needs, including shifting resources to a newly identified critical/high-need foreign language.

The Ohio University language survey results indicate that Ohio's suburbanites are more likely to support foreign language education than residents of urban and rural areas, but that a large segment of the state's population does not believe foreign language ability brings job opportunities. With Ohio's industrial cities in decline and agriculture competing globally for markets, the demographics that most need new paths to profitability are the groups least cognizant of the benefits of foreign language skills. The LPL will be an excellent medium through which success stories involving foreign-language speaking Ohioans can be shared with state decision makers in business and government. Anecdotal and qualitative data relating foreign language skills to increased business and happier immigrant populations already exist, but they lack a group like LPL to disseminate them.

*Which organizations might be the drivers for this project?*

The Ohio International Trade Division, as a representative of the state's export interests, will be interested in the LPL's ability to find/create opportunities for its constituents. The Ohio Tourist Office will find this organization helpful in developing tourism from abroad. The Ohio Chamber of Commerce and trade associations will expand their foreign resources. The Ohio Department of Education will have access to an organization of advocates and advisors for their future foreign language policies. Ohio's heritage communities and international organizations will have an umbrella organization through which their concerns can be amplified.

*What would be the timeframe for establishing such an organization?*

It will take two years to organize membership, drawing on the databases organized by the Ohio LCSC. After that, it will take two to three years to build committed partnerships and develop a strategic plan for advancing the LPL's goals.

*How does the LPL contribute to the Strategic Vision?*

Many individuals and organizations already share the strategic vision for Ohio's future, but do not know there are others like them in the state. The LPL can provide the focus on language and culture and provide the social vehicle for articulating problems and working toward solutions. Handled correctly, this organization can be a desirable affiliation for the individuals and organizations that are or are intending to play on the global stage.

In addition to articulating problems, the LPL also articulates success stories of Ohioans using foreign language skills in their careers, generating demand for more such individuals and pushing a virtuous cycle of foreign language supply and demand.

## B. Developing Educational Models and Resources for Lifetime Foreign Language Learning and Teaching

The strategy for assuring that the next generation of Ohioans will be players in the global competition for economic and cultural advantage should focus on making effective language instruction available across the state and in providing motivation for developing and maintaining high-level language abilities. The Design Teams suggested tactics for seeing that strategy to a successful conclusion. Dovetailing with FLAC recommendations, some tactics will require political allocations of scarce resources, some will only require us to rethink current practices and consider the redirection of current resources to more effective use.

## Action Item 3: Developing Long Sequences of Foreign Language Study

The long-term goal is to establish extensive articulated programs of instruction in critical languages. Depending on the capacities of local communities, such programs should begin in the early elementary grades. If such sequences are not available in certain languages at lower levels, then institutions of higher education should institute extended sequences of language instruction focused on developing students who are capable of functioning in career environments, even if these sequences must extend into graduate levels to achieve these goals. The longer the sequence, the better.

For producing high-ability graduates, the length of time students are exposed to *quality* language training is the best indicator of consistently achieving success. Many education institutions in Asia and Europe are opting for a full K-16 sequence, with the role of dual-language schools becoming increasingly important. The one feature of sequential years of foreign language study that cannot be ignored is that the sequence must lead to continued study. A K-12 program should not be attempted unless there is intention and commitment to continue the entire sequence and encourage graduates to continue their use of the language in college, in their work, or by spending time in countries where the language is spoken. Based on Ohio's current and anticipated foreign language needs, languages that should be taught in extended sequences include (in alphabetical order): Arabic, Chinese, French, German, Japanese, and Russian. Different localities around Ohio may have reasons for including other languages in this list. Here are some tactics for realizing these extended sequences of foreign language study in schools across Ohio.

*Regional focus on particular languages:* Supporting an extended sequence of foreign language study is a significant commitment for any school or school system; therefore, the choice of which language sequence should be adopted is critical. For the state of Ohio, it would be beneficial if different communities focused on different languages, perhaps based on the availability of language resources in that community. Toledo would find extensive resources for developing an Arabic sequence, Central Ohio would find reasons for focusing on Chinese and Japanese, and the Cleveland area would find local resources for choosing to develop sequences in Russian and Eastern European languages. Refer to the following chart to see a regional distribution of immigrants in Ohio. Please note that Arabic speakers seem to be left out of this chart.

*Materials development for early foreign language education in less-commonly-taught languages:* There is a severe shortage of teaching materials for use in elementary and middle schools, especially for the so-called "less commonly taught languages" such as Japanese, Chinese, Arabic, Farsi, Korean. A concerted effort is necessary to produce the multimedia materials numerous enough to provide instructors with a choice. For early childhood learning materials, there is a need for language and culture experts to join forces with early childhood learning experts to create the most effective learning environments for pre-K through fifth grade learners. Since these sets of expertise usually reside in different parts of the major universities that are not accustomed to working together, institutional leadership must encourage these kinds of cooperative projects to be undertaken.

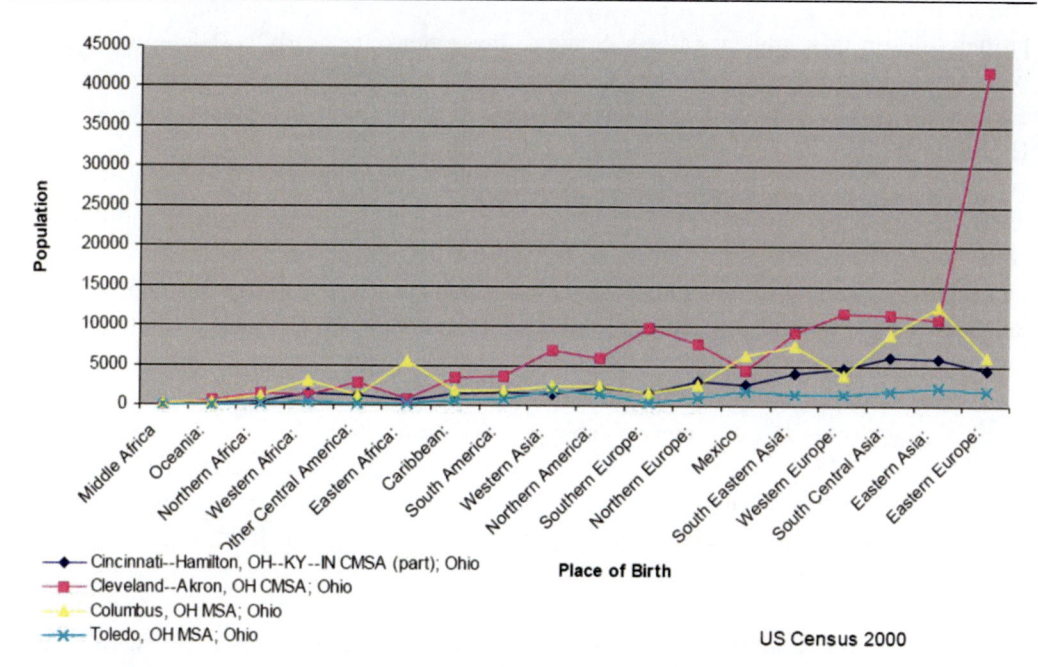

From: The Ohio State University Ohio Agricultural Research and Development Center, www.farmtomarkets.com/marketinfo/Organic%20OH%20Proud%20Foods.pdf

Ohio Immigrant Population by Metropolitan Area and Region of Birth (2000)

*Integration of foreign language education and content education:* Language, unlike technical areas like math and history, can be used as a medium for communication rather than just a subject itself. Research shows that advanced levels of foreign language ability are only reached when learners are able to use the language as a medium of exchange in a particular field. Educational institutions can take advantage of these findings and integrate foreign language education with other fields of knowledge: mathematics, science, technology, public policy, or engineering. The end result should be students who can work in the languages they have studied. For example, one American who learned Chinese and earned an MBA in the US now oversees a Chinese factory for its American owners. Being bilingual and bicultural, the American is able to communicate American business needs to the Chinese factory in a way that makes sense to the Chinese while at the same time explaining the Chinese employees' needs and concerns to the US.

Integrated subject and foreign language education can be found in immersion schools, dual-language schools, languages for special purposes courses, and **internships. In Columbus'** K-8 French immersion school Ecole Kenwood, students already receive 50% of their instruction in French by grade 5; at the Ohio State University, Chinese Flagship Program graduate students work with Chinese mentors to complete practical research in their major. Copying such programs in more places, in more languages and in more grades, Ohio can assume the lead in American schools by shifting the role of foreign language instruction in the overall educational process.

*Supplying motivations for studying in extended sequences of foreign language instruction:* There are many ways to encourage students to achieve high-level language proficiencies in their student careers. Some of these steps are nearly cost-free, while others will require institutions to allocate significant resources. An example of the former is the acknowledgment of achievement of foreign language proficiency on diplomas and transcripts. High school diplomas could **acknowledge a demonstrated ability in** "**advanced**" **language (a** foreign language and English) and universities **could acknowledge the** "**superior**" **level of ability in language**. This would require schools to consider foreign language ability on par with honors designations. A more costly acknowledgement of achievement in foreign languages would be a tuition rebate for college graduates who can **demonstrate** "**superior**" language competence. Such rebates could be adjusted to reward achievement in critical languages more generously than achievement in more widely studied languages. A 10% to 20% rebate on tuition would be powerful enough to increase the number of students graduating with the desired language abilities. Governments and private industry can also establish scholarships to support students who are studying both a foreign language and an employable skill. For example, there could be a Proctor & Gamble scholarship for Spanish Marketing awarded to a student who creates a Spanish-language marketing strategy that bridges to Latino consumers.

*Study Abroad, Community Service and Internships:* Through sister city partnerships, corporate relations with foreign operations, individual connections, university development and alumni offices, opportunities can be developed in foreign communities for students and graduates of extended sequence programs to develop working experiences in their languages of study. For example, the University of **Dayton's School of Engineering could ask its** counterpart in sister city Augsburg, Germany to help arrange internships for German-speaking mechanical engineering students at leading German truck and engine maker MAN Diesel.

*What are the desired outcomes of the extended sequences of foreign language study in Ohio schools?*

Basing foreign language study on extended sequences acknowledges the nature of the process of learning to communicate in a foreign language. Researchers show that socialization **in one's own culture** takes from 25,000 to 35,000 hours of intimate interactions with doting caregivers; becoming socialized **in both one's own culture and a second culture is** an ongoing endeavor that will be nurtured and encouraged by extended sequences. By the time our students reach college, they can be in a position to learn to perform professional tasks in their chosen foreign languages. If a student has learned to speak general-use Spanish by the time of high school graduate, s/he can learn, for example, engineering Spanish in college. A tier-1 auto parts supplier recently brought a Mexican engineer to a plant in Ohio to improve communications after discovering that his American predecessor was unable to break the culture barrier and failed to communicate the needs of customers GM and Ford to plants in Mexico. Ohioans (including Hispanic-American Ohioans) trained in professional engineering Spanish would have been able to resolve the communication problems without the supplier having to move the Mexican engineer, his wife and their three children to Ohio.

An integral part of achieving professional ability in foreign language environments is having practical training in the form of internships. Americans on internships abroad will learn how to apply their classroom achievements to the specific environments of their target cultures. Through the former US/China Links program and now the Chinese Flagship graduate program, Ohio State University students of Chinese have been placed in 5+ month internships in China where they have learned how to entertain Chinese cruise ship guests, attract foreign investment, produce Chinese television shows, and create financial reports. Many forms of knowledge can only be acquired through experience, and internships abroad will inculcate Americans with experiential knowledge while reinforcing their foreign language abilities.

*Which organizations might be the drivers for establishing extended sequences of language study?*

It will be necessary for the Ohio Department of Education to promulgate the practice of regional language emphasis. The US Department of Education can direct resources to extended-sequence programs. The US Departments of Defense, Commerce and Labor will be interested in the impact this will have on workforce development. The Ohio Board of Regents, Ohio university presidents, university deans and department chairs, and university development offices will see the advantages of combining foreign language study with academic and career goals. Local school systems will develop special expertise in particular languages, with Columbus creating programs to teach Somali and Toledo to teach Arabic. Private foundations with educational and international missions will view these reforms as models for the rest of the country. Publishers of educational materials in the US and in the countries of the languages being studied will see extended sequences as an expanding market for their products.

*What would be the timeframe for establishing extended sequences of foreign language study in Ohio schools?*

  i.   Articulated early FL education: 7-8 years (based on FLAC estimates)
  ii.  Materials development: 5-10 years
  iii. Integration of foreign language and academic subjects: 5-10 years
  iv.  Scholarships and rebates for language proficiency: 1-3 years
  v.   Acknowledgements of language proficiency: Immediately
  vi.  Internships: Immediately

*How would extended sequences contribute to the Strategic Vision?*

Establishing extended sequences of foreign language study that are integrated with other academic and technical subjects will cause a paradigm shift in foreign language education. The Design Teams consider this a necessity if the needs identified by the Language Summit are to be met. It will take the entire education system to produce individuals ready to work in foreign language environments—from the political will to focus on foreign language capacity as a workforce issue, to the strategic educational decisions to focus on particular languages and academic levels, to the daily implementation of performance-based instruction. Whether the individual is in Ohio working with foreign language speakers or is in a foreign land as a representative of an Ohio organization, the skills necessary for interacting with foreign language speakers on their terms require more time to acquire than any single educational institution can provide. For this reason, the Design Teams again agree with FLAC that articulation across all levels of education is the only viable and scalable means of consistently producing Ohioans who can use world languages in all aspects of their personal and work lives.

**Action Item 4: Train, license and employ more teachers educated in the use of technology and develop networked programs around these qualified teachers**

Especially when FLAC and Design Team recommendations for extended sequences of foreign language study are implemented across the state, there will be many more positions for foreign language teachers than there are currently individuals qualified to fill those positions. Growth in Spanish enrollments are driving the need for trained language educators in Ohio, but the creation of entirely new less-commonly taught language programs is also pointing the state toward a severe shortage of well-trained foreign language teachers.

One solution to the problem has been the establishment of the Governor's Alternative Licensure Program (ALP). Created to fill teacher shortages across a number of subjects, the ALP has seen mixed results in producing qualified instructors that are immediately hired. For languages with broad appeal like French and Spanish, the positive results of the ALP are clear. Under traditional licensure procedures, 25 institutions of higher education produced about 225 language teachers per year. In one cohort, ALP produced 120 qualified language instructors.

Because of their popularity with students and administrators, there is a shortage of teachers for French and Spanish programs across the state, but there is also dire need for qualified teachers of "critical languages" such as Chinese, Arabic and Farsi. This shortfall has many causes: few schools hire such teachers, few training programs produce such teachers and there are few authorized programs granting teaching licenses in these languages. While the need for fully certified teachers of critical languages looms large in the minds of the participants in the Language Summit and the Design Teams, the lack of demand and supply has made it difficult to move in that direction.

The Governor's Alternative Licensure Program in languages such as Arabic, Chinese, and Japanese was an attempt to break this stalemate. This program produced a few dozen trainees qualified for certification, mostly in Chinese. However, only a few of these individuals were hired by Ohio schools. One reason was the availability of volunteer, or "free," teachers from China, provided by the Office of the Chinese Language Council International through the College Board and other cooperating agencies. These volunteers seemed to diminish the market for the Chinese teachers trained in Ohio who are qualified for licensure. This experience shows us that the state must have an overall policy for developing the human resources to meet its long-term needs. The opportune grasping at all available solutions can easily develop into harmful contradictions that impede the development of the infrastructure necessary for making Ohio a leader in foreign language education.

The first step toward creating an overall language teacher training policy is to start a campaign to convince Ohio educators to build substantial language programs in their schools. Then develop the supply chain by:

1. Developing more high quality, accelerated teacher training programs for high-need, critical languages
2. Establishing more regular teacher training programs in universities and private training centers
3. Recruiting college educated heritage speakers to become licensed teachers of critical languages

4.  Training teachers how to use technology creatively and effectively in foreign language instruction.

As the need for qualified foreign language teachers reaches a critical stage, departments of education may consider programs that offer subsidies to schools for hiring qualified teachers. Such subsidies could have time limits and be offered with the understanding that the local school will continue successful foreign language programs.

As we develop a corps of qualified teachers in critical languages, Ohio should think outside the box and create a series of language courses that are accessible through the Internet. We should strive to provide the widest range of Ohio students with opportunities to study the languages they want to learn. Even if a school or school district offers an extended sequence of language courses, it cannot do so for more than one or two languages. However, it could make other possibilities available to students if qualified teachers are connected to students in schools throughout the state by means of the Internet and other instructional technologies. Examples of such networked programs are the Regents Chinese Academy (summer 2007) and the Distance Chinese Individualized Instruction Program at Ohio State.

*What are the desired outcomes of having qualified teachers and networked programs?*

The primary goal of increased teacher training and the creation of multi-school programs is to accelerate the state's capacity to teach foreign languages. While it is not practical for every school in every school district to have different teachers for all the target languages, different districts can focus on specific languages and offer other languages through the Internet. As many experts have pointed out, learning a second foreign language is easier than learning a first one; thus, students who happen to live in a district with elementary school Russian are not fated to learning only Russian in their lives – they may pick up a different language later on in their student career as they attend schools with other options or qualify for a networked program.

A standardized teacher licensure program will lead to growth in teacher programs and a greater number of licensed teachers. Because foreign language education will become integrated with subject teaching, teacher training will have to include team teaching skills so that foreign language teachers-to-be become comfortable with and effective in having a supporting role in subject learning. As language proficiencies spread and subject-matter teachers are imported (virtually or actually) from other countries to teach their subjects in American schools, the licensure processes will need to be streamlined and made less burdensome on potential teachers.

With technology employed in the classroom and beyond, we can integrate current internet and television content into language instruction, have students interact with foreign nationals in the target language in speech and writing, and use videoconferencing technologies to take foreign language education to areas of Ohio that would otherwise be unable to provide early or varied foreign language education choices.

Having networked programs would allow small groups of students interested in studying a language not offered locally to combine with similar groups across the state and form complete language classes. Thus, isolated students of a language can participate in a fully resourced course under a qualified instructor. Networked programs could include the idea of creating multi-school classrooms and global connections between Ohio classrooms and classrooms throughout the world.

*Which organizations might be the drivers for having qualified teachers and networked programs?*

The Ohio Department of Education, in cooperation with university schools of education, and with organizational support from FLAC, can simplify certification processes. Interstate teacher associations can develop agreements on accepting certification between states. Private teacher training schools can offer training programs based on the published standards for certification. Heritage community organizations can identify and encourage qualified individuals to become certified teachers. Local school districts can offer wider choices to their students.

*What would be the timeframe for having qualified teachers and networked programs?*

It will take two years to create accelerated teacher certification programs based on existing ones (e.g., accelerated Arabic, Japanese and Chinese alternative licensure programs at Ohio State, the University of Findlay and Cleveland State). It will take another three years to establish new teacher training programs for critical languages in schools of education throughout the state. It will take an undetermined number of years to change federal policies regarding visa requirements so that more heritage speakers are eligible to matriculate into these programs (e.g., spouses of international students). It will take two years to develop instructional materials describing use of technology in the classroom. Clusters of networked programs can be set up within one year.

*How would having qualified teachers and networked programs contribute to the strategic vision?*

Without qualified teachers, students cannot learn foreign languages. As foreign language education programs increase in quantity and the expectations for proficiency rise across the country, standardized teacher qualifications and certification will contribute to articulation across grades, across localities, and even across languages. Even with a host of extra-curricular learning opportunities available to learners of all ages (from watching foreign cartoons to internships), qualified foreign language teachers are necessary for leading the language learning experience.

Networked programs under the direction of qualified teachers can extend language learning opportunities throughout the state, bringing the economic and security benefits (e.g., smooth interaction with public services) to members of all Ohio communities.

### Action Item 5: Create performance-based tools for assessing foreign language learners' ability to communicate effectively

Assessment instruments for identifying an individual's skill and task proficiencies in a given language and a program's effectiveness are key to the development of the infrastructure that will sustain this effort. Once the goal of language study is determined to be the ability to work in the language, performance-based assessments can provide standards for language proficiency and language teaching qualifications. The LCSC can assemble and distribute currently available assessment instruments (e.g., OPI, STAMP test, CAAP tests, NOELLA, SOPI), as well as create new assessment instruments using the latest technology and pedagogical research. In the Internet age, assessments can be implemented from any location and databases maintained to identify persons and organizations with language and teaching qualifications.

*What are the desired outcomes of reliable performance-based assessments in foreign language study?*

If performance-based tests and portfolio assessments reflect whether or not students are able to use foreign language skills to communicate with foreign counterparts, teachers who are inclined to "teach to the test" will emphasize performance in their instruction. If progressing to higher levels of instruction is tied to performance in the target culture, as sports is tied to the playing fields and music to the recital hall, students will clearly understand the nature of learning to communicate in a foreign language.

Effective assessment will require the creation of third-party assessment agencies. Assessment should not be controlled by the schools or programs that teach the languages. Bureaucracies responsible for evaluating their own achievements tend to report success. Also, independent assessments will make it possible to compare language programs across schools and regions which will facilitate the improvement of language instruction in general. With commonly-accepted standards for assessment in place, third party assessors can be tasked to assess foreign language programs and their learners throughout the state.

*Which organizations might be the drivers for creating effective assessment tools?*

Under this plan, the Ohio and US Departments of Education will be key in establishing the need for effective and assessment instruments. The American Council on the Teaching of Foreign Languages (ACTFL), as the current standard-bearer of language proficiency, will play a role in developing broader assessment tools. The Departments of Defense and State, including the Interagency Language Roundtable, will play an important role in the use and validation of such assessment tools. Language-based and subject-based teaching associations will contribute to creating content-appropriate standards.

*What would be the timeframe for establishing reliable assessment for language study?*

In conjunction with the development of organizations such as the Ohio LCSC, an assessment center could be partially operational within three years and fully operational in five years.

*How would reliable assessment instruments contribute to the Strategic vision?*

Effective assessment tools are necessary in order to measure progress toward realizing the goals of creating a multilingual workforce and developing the educational programs necessary to doing that.

The Roadmap Design Teams' recommendations were reached after several weeks of reviewing data and discussing the current state of foreign language education and use in Ohio. The following sections contextualize the environment in which the preceding recommendations were born, describing Ohio's level of globalization from a statistical perspective as well as Ohio's current foreign language capacity strengths and weaknesses.

## IV. The Current State of Play

### Overview

Thanks to its strong manufacturing and agricultural base and well-established higher education system, Ohio is currently a highly internationalized state:

- 20.6% of Ohio manufacturing jobs are linked to exports, mostly in vehicles and machinery
- Ohio's agricultural export volume was 13th in the nation in 2005 and 6th in soybean exports
- Ohio ranks #7 in non-bank foreign direct investment and 8th in # of foreign direct investment jobs
- Ohio's international students rank ninth in the nation in their economic contribution to the state (tuition, living expenses, etc)
- Ohio agriculture depends on immigrant labor for harvesting and milking. At last count, 15,782 migrant laborers worked in Ohio.
- The top countries with businesses in Ohio are: Japan (339), Germany (165) and Canada (129)

Ohio's aggregate success in internationalization also reflects the migration of manufacturing jobs—once Ohio's backbone—to Canada, Mexico and Asia. While Ohio corporations have benefited from off-shoring goods and services, Ohio's workers have seen their opportunities decline. The data below describes Ohio's needs for greater internationalization in such areas as labor management and tourism:

- Only 3% of documented Ohio residents were born outside the United States… but that number (and another possible 75,000 undocumented immigrants) is greater than the population of Cincinnati
- Only 7.3% of the labor force in the Midwest is foreign born… but immigrants accounted for 83% of labor force growth here
- 18,465 interpretations were performed in Ohio courts 2003-2004… but 30% of court interpreters have not been required to provide qualification of their skill
- Canadians comprise the largest group of international visitors to Ohio, with German- and English-speaking Europeans following – all of whom speak languages already commonly spoken by Ohioans
- The #1 destination for Ohio State students studying abroad is England. Numbers 6, 9 and 10 are also English-based programs in English-speaking locations

### *The Private Sector and Foreign Languages*

As far as Ohio business is concerned, the issue is not how many foreign language majors Ohio's education system produces every year, but how many graduates are ready to *work* in foreign language environments. In the absence of Spanish-speaking accountants or Chinese-speaking mechanical engineers, large Ohio companies prefer to rely on US-educated natives of the target culture – and large budgets – to cross the cultural barrier. Smaller employers cannot afford to spend large amounts of money to resolve cross-cultural communication problems, but also cannot afford to hire the few employees who have mastered both a technical specialty and foreign language skills.

The labor market for professionally-skilled foreign language speakers in Ohio presents a chicken-and-egg problem: there are very few potential employees who are technically skilled and speak a foreign language at advanced levels, so employers are satisfied with only technical skill; students see that foreign language skill does not make them any more competitive and so they do not pursue the difficult road of mastering a foreign language and a technical skill.

As one Ohio State foreign language major discovered, many American jobs situated in foreign language environments are expatriate assignments reserved for middle and upper level management. Even students who have majored in a technical field and achieved a high level of foreign language ability before graduating are faced with the prospect of having to work for ten years in non-foreign language-using positions before they can even be considered for expatriate assignment.

### Foreign Language Use and the Public Sector

For the most part, Ohio government offices' foreign language needs lie in serving the Latinos that comprise a large portion of the state's agricultural workforce. Following Spanish, other top language needs encountered by Ohio government offices include: Somali, Arabic, Russian, Chinese, and Vietnamese. Spanish is far and away the most-needed foreign language in Ohio's public sector.

Due to Title VI requirements to make government services available regardless of citizens' English skills, various Ohio offices have taken steps to translate and interpret commonly-encountered materials. In 2003, Ohio courts spent $982,000 on over 18,000 court interpretations; the Ohio Department of Jobs and Family Services has Spanish-speaking staff to interact with immigrant constituents; Ohio law enforcement officials have available to them cards that say "I need an interpreter for [language X]" in case they encounter a language barrier.

Interpretation and translation is generally provided by private third parties, some of whom hold qualifications for their languages skills, but many of whom do not, relying only on their work experience to demonstrate their ability. Some Ohio offices also rely on heritage speakers such as Latino-Americans to interact with members of the target community.

### Foreign Language Education

According to the American Council of Teachers of Foreign Languages, foreign language enrollment in Ohio outgrew foreign language enrollment across the nation as a whole. A 2002 Modern Language Association report showed that pre-college foreign language enrollments in the Midwest compared favorably to other regions of the nation, with Spanish enrollment second only to the South Atlantic, French enrollment third behind the South Atlantic and Northeast and German and Japanese enrollments well ahead of all other regions in the country.

Few Ohio schools offer foreign languages for elementary students. In a few instances Arabic, Chinese, Japanese, German, French, Spanish, Russian, are offered at the kindergarten level… but only about 4,500 kindergarten students in all of Ohio received any language instruction in 2005-2006, compared to nearly 87,000 high school sophomores. These languages and Hebrew, Greek, Latin, Swahili, and Polish are all offered in the public schools, but as is common across the country, the most popular languages remain Spanish, French and German.

Nationally, the top five world languages by enrollment are, in order: Spanish, French, German, Italian and Japanese. In Ohio, the popular world languages were: Spanish, French, German, Latin and Italian.

For most public school students in Ohio, there simply are no other alternatives to studying French, German or Spanish

## V. Gap Analysis of Ohio's Current State of Play

Ohio has a number of assets that promote the study and use of foreign languages amongst its citizens; and like any other state, Ohio faces many obstacles to improving the current foreign language learning situation. In this section, we offer an analysis of the strengths, weaknesses, opportunities and threats regarding Ohio's ability to improve its citizens' ability to interact with people for whom English is not their first language.

### *Strengths*

### Education

Ohio's education system stands out amongst all its other strengths. In addition to having an excellent network of primary and secondary schools, Ohio is home to many well-respected universities. In addition to four-year institutions, Ohio has many forward-looking community colleges that are geared toward practical education and serve populations that want to see a direct relationship between their education and their work.

Eleven of Ohio's 13 public universities offer foreign language majors and Ohio universities sent nearly 9,000 students on study abroad programs in the 2004/2005 school year. Within our borders, the Ohio State University is home to Chinese Flagship programs for K-16 Chinese education and beyond as well as home to a Title-VI-funded Center for International Business Education and Research (CIBER) and the National East Asian Languages Resource Center. With few Ohioans more than 75 miles away from some institution of higher learning, Ohio has an excellent existing system through which foreign language/culture outreach can be conducted.

Perhaps because Ohio has so many universities, some of them recognize that they must be innovative in order to compete. One consulting firm in Cleveland, China Source Link, is working with the University of Akron to develop foreign language certification for students in technical majors. Graduates in such fields as engineering and architecture will be tested and awarded proficiency certificates that they can show to potential employers and justify the salaries that bilinguals with technical skills should earn.

As numerous as Ohio's universities are, its rural citizens are spread over a large territory. Universities like Ohio State are taking a leading role in offering foreign language distance education to rural communities. Through distance education, learners in otherwise isolated communities are beginning to enjoy top-notch foreign language instruction.

Another important strength of Ohio's universities is their international student population. In the 2005/2006 school year, Ohio universities had the 9th highest number of international students of all 50 states. The students not only contribute to the local economy, but their very presence internationalizes discussion in class and helps Ohio students learn to work with people from very different backgrounds. When they graduate, these students also provide Ohio with a ready population of bilingual workers with technical skill.

Though higher education has traditionally been the center of attention for foreign language study, it is becoming clear that training for professionally-useful levels of foreign language proficiency should start earlier for some languages and *must* start earlier for several others (i.e., Arabic, Japanese, Korean and Chinese). Ohio is a nationally-recognized leader in pre-college foreign language education, and its legislature recently put its weight behind "early" foreign language education by passing House Bill 115, which provides funds for a variety of foreign language learning programs, from the summer Regents Academy for foreign languages to alternative teacher licensure programs for accelerated qualification of teachers in critical languages. House Bill 115 also created the Foreign Language Advisory Council (FLAC), a body whose Ohio Department of Education representative, Dr. Deborah Robinson, was also a Roadmap Design Team member. Demonstrating the high-level collaboration that is now taking place in Ohio foreign language education, FLAC and Roadmap Design Team outcomes are being shared between each other.

On a local basis, Ohio schools are experimenting with varying models of early foreign language education, from immersion (Columbus City Schools), partial immersion (Cincinnati) to dual immersion (Cleveland Buhrer Elementary), to content-related language instruction (Toledo Larchmont and Grove Patterson). In addition to foreign language education, some Ohio students are also taking International Baccalaureate courses that stress knowledge of the world.

Finally, Ohio's growing immigrant communities have established numerous "heritage schools" where the second generation is taught the language and culture of their homelands. Ohio's Chinese heritage schools are particularly well-known and respected; Toledo's large Muslim community has also established a weekend Arabic school (Al Bayan) whose enrollment increases necessitated the addition of a new wing.

## Tradition and Diversity

An important aspect of Ohio's strength in cross-cultural interaction is, as Cleveland businesswoman Kimberly Kirkendall says, "Midwestern values export well". Many Ohioans are brought up valuing community and family relationships and hard work, values that are shared with most cultures around the world. Ohio's special combination of urban areas (Cleveland, Akron, Youngstown, Toledo, Dayton, Columbus, Cincinnati) and rural areas has produced a state in which you find city people with traditional values, values very similar to those held by people from the developing nations with which Ohioans do business and from where Ohio's agricultural labor comes.

Though 97% of Ohioans were born in the US, there is still a great amount of diversity in the state, especially in urban areas. From Toledo's Arab community to Cleveland's Russians, from Columbus' Somali community to Cincinnati's South Asians, the amount of ethnic diversity in the state is increasingly significant. Add to that Columbus' status as having one of the nation's largest gay communities, many Ohioans are used to diversity of cultures and viewpoints. Because of Ohio's ethnic diversity, organizations have arisen to serve their needs and to help them integrate into American society. Organizations such as Asian American Community Services, Community Refugee and Immigrant Services, the Ohio Hispanic Coalition and the Spanish American Committee are existing centers of cross-cultural skill and interaction. These and other heritage organizations produce foreign language media, offer English classes, and often serve as small-scale clearing houses for expertise in the respective cultures they represent (including interpreters).

## Business & Government Infrastructure

An important strength that Ohio has in terms of foreign language ability is the degree to which Ohio businesses and government offices interact with peoples for whom English is not their native language.

From GE aircraft engines from Cincinnati to bovine semen from northwest Ohio, Ohio's long-standing experience in the export of manufactured goods and agriculture products has put Ohio business on the front lines of cross-cultural interaction for decades. Ohio's strong financial and high-tech sectors are also exporting services around the globe. Despite huge job losses from NAFTA in the 1990's, Ohio has managed to remain competitive on the world market. Supporting this growth is an active state Department of Development whose domestic initiatives are led by the Office of Workforce Development, and whose export promotion is led by the International Trade Division.

Over 20% of Ohio's manufacturing jobs are export-related, but the state's international business is far from limited to exporting American goods. With its strong base in the auto and machinery industries, Ohio has attracted large amounts of foreign direct investment from Japan and Germany[3]. With so much cross-border and cross-culture business taking place with Ohioans, there is a fair degree of recognition that Ohio's future is closely tied to its ability to remain a part of the global community.

Ohio's multicultural strength in business and government is not limited to international trade, however. With a growing immigrant population, Ohio government offices and businesses are quickly finding ways of working with and capitalizing on the immigrant influx. Immigrants with different dietary standards are creating a need for more "organic" foods and specific methods of livestock harvesting perfectly suited to Ohio's modest-sized agricultural operations. Ohio's Department of Jobs and Family Services (ODJFS) is also working hard to make sure that the immigrant workers that keep the state's agricultural economy going are taken care of to the fullest extent of the law. With federal support, ODJFS administers "One-stops" state-wide, where employers and potential employers are encouraged to find one another and to engage in training programs that enable each side to work better with the other.

## *Weaknesses*

## Education & Educational Resources

Ohio's greatest strength is also its greatest weakness in achieving widespread and/or high-level foreign language proficiency. While there are pockets of experimentation with early foreign language education, for the most part, they are the exceptions that prove the rule: primary foreign language education in Ohio is limited and never mandatory.

There is insufficient funding to support training, licensure and/or employment of the number of foreign language teachers required to make foreign language learning common throughout the state. In many school districts, the need for foreign language instruction is not even apparent to their administrators. Among schools that have foreign language classes, they are not articulated with higher education, leading to wasteful re-learning when and if students reach college. Other schools may offer foreign language instruction for a year or two, but cannot provide continuous learning opportunities from the time of initial instruction through high school graduation.

One factor contributing to Ohio's weakness in pre-college foreign language education is the relative lack of non-traditional learning opportunities; foreign language learning for most children remains a somewhat stale and abstract exercise that involves neither interaction with natives of the target culture nor even interaction with an instructor that has spent significant time in-country. Local Ohio businesses, which are interacting with native speakers of foreign languages all the time are not connected to education and are ignored as resources for foreign language education and practice.

Because education in Ohio is locally regulated, there is a lack of coordination between foreign language instructors, resources and administrators that leads to duplicated work as well as regions of minimal coverage. Some languages have a wealth of teaching materials, while others have very little, especially for primary and secondary school learners. Without interregional cooperation, individual discoveries of useful teaching materials often remain local.

Finally – and this is a systemic and conceptual problem – foreign language education in Ohio is often divorced from the practical applications that foreign language skill must have in order to be relevant. Few schools – at any level – relate foreign language use to technical skill; international business programs do not require more than a year or two of a foreign language – hardly enough for professional proficiency in most languages; math and engineering programs do not help students find ways of incorporating foreign language study in already tightly-packed curricula; high school students are often taught foreign languages as if they were learning to be children in the target culture, rather than adults-to-be. While there are inchoative movements toward developing a foreign language policy for the state, the present situation has yet to be significantly influenced by these initiatives.

## Public Attitudes

There remains a belief in Ohio that we have done very well using English only, and so our foreign language ability is not as important as everyone else's ability to learn English. Xenophobia and an "English-only" sentiment are common throughout the state, even in urban areas. Internationally, it is often felt that foreigners doing business with Ohio *should* speak English, while domestically, immigrants are expected to assimilate and give up many trappings of their native cultures. Particularly in communities where Hispanic laborers are many, the win-win arrangement of having this population in Ohio – cheaper labor, social security payments that support Americans, cultural diversity – is not recognized.

As a rust-belt state, Ohio is home to many blue-collar workers who understand that their jobs were lost to capital shifted to Canada, Mexico, and Asia. Because the savings/wealth generated by lower manufacturing costs do not trickle down to laid-off line workers, many working class Ohioans blame globalization and foreign-language speaking communities for their economic hardship. To people for whom "work" means "factory work," foreign language learning is sometimes perceived as "selling out" or helping to move even more jobs overseas rather than creating previously unexplored opportunities for employment.

Many Ohioans do not accept the utility of foreign language ability, but sometimes even those who do often fail to realize the amount of time and resources that are required to achieve foreign language skills at a professionally-useful level. A couple years of foreign language instruction may "build character" and certainly goes a long way toward opening young minds to the possibility of alternative world views and lifeways, but a couple years of nearly any language is woefully insufficient for practical employment.

Added together, the fear of foreigners, fear of the unknown, and fear of the difficulty of language learning contribute to a general lack of respect for foreign language learning in many parts of the state. In a vicious cycle, local governments do not fund foreign language education and so learners grow up in monocultural environments, continuing to fear and misunderstand foreignness; these learners then become businesspeople and policy makers who again give foreign language education short-shrift. With few models of what Ohioans with foreign language experience can do, few are prepared to make the sacrifices necessary for foreign language education to expand at the grass roots level.

The major media outlets of the state are not focused on international issues or on the challenges facing Ohio in the global arena. Treatments of events and people beyond the borders of the state and nation have a distant focus and are mostly confined to wire reports or network feeds. The roles of Ohioans in the world at large and foreigners in Ohio are usually beneath the media radar. Ohioans who achieve notable things abroad are not noticed. Programs that represent Ohio in distant parts of the planet do not attract the attention of reporters and their editors. Like the weather that stops at the national borders on television weather reports, the winds of change from foreign sources do not make it into shallow waters of public discourse in Ohio. Without a change in the attitudes toward international issues and the opportunities offered by expanding language and culture capacity on the part of those who control the media in Ohio, a change in public attitudes will continue to be a daunting challenge.

### *Opportunities*

Ohio also has many institutional and human resources that can be further mobilized to support foreign language education. There are sources of government funding that could be taken advantage of, and groups involved in similar endeavors can begin working together. The fact that Ohio's opportunities are so numerous bodes well for progress in the immediate and distant futures.

#### *Preschool-16 education*

Ohio has a number of brand-new programs for foreign language/culture education as well as areas in which existing resources have not yet been utilized.

The new Chinese Flagship Program at Ohio State and new Confucius Institute at Miami University are both contributing to the expansion of Chinese education in Ohio with programs to support K-16+ language instruction as well as cross-cultural exchanges. The University of Findlay, a school that has long been ahead of the curve in international cooperation, offers a bilingual business degree that can be a model for other universities. The University of Akron is exploring language certification for non-language majors to demonstrate their skill to potential employees. Ohio's newly-formed Foreign Language Advisory Committee is in a position to help align these various initiatives.

With the internet available throughout the state, technology can be used to bring foreign language education to everyone. New ways in which technology can be used for foreign language education include integration of satellite TV programs in course content, integrating the Internet and language classes, expanding use of videoconferencing technology for distance learning, and finding ways to use video games as a constructive language learning tool (i.e., online community games like Second Life and World of Warcraft).

An important opportunity that has yet to be taken advantage of is K-16 articulation. Language learning is a long-term endeavor, so it is important that students are able to take language classes year after year without unnecessary interruptions or repetition. Because and K-12 and post-secondary schools are governed by state agencies, it has been difficult to create a smooth learning transition from high school to college. The creation of FLAC promises to help bridge this gap.

Finally, non-traditional language learning delivery systems can be further developed and promoted. These include distance learning between hub and spoke schools (i.e. between cities and rural communities), greater integration of private language instruction and the school system (i.e., use of complementary materials, exchange of ideas and methods), greater use of the language magnet school concept (each state could have a handful of language magnet schools devoted to learning certain languages), and integration of foreign language study and technical skills (such as math and science programs, nursing/health, and business).

*Government support*

There is a fair amount of funding available for cross-cultural activities in Ohio, but its existence is often unknown. Programs such as the Workforce Investment Act (WIA) and the Federal Department of Labor's Workforce Innovation in Regional Economic Development (WIRED) could be taken advantage of more to integrate immigrant communities; faith-based initiatives are another source of funding that has not been tapped for language/culture outreach. Federally-funded Title VI area studies centers at universities have been excellent loci for academic exchange, but they could go further to integrate foreign language/culture knowledge in average Ohioans' daily lives.

Even though there may be untapped funds at the federal and local level that could be used for language/culture education, it seems that many government employees themselves are unaware of the benefits of cross-cultural understanding. Government offices could do more to increase compliance with Title VI requirements regarding providing services in foreign languages; government employees could receive more *relevant* multicultural training so as to prevent discrimination in the workplace.

Another important opportunity is the fact that Ohio is a key election state with a new governor. With so many eyes on Ohio, the state is in a good situation to do something to make itself stand out. With a new president, the Ohio State University is in a similar position.

*Community Culture Centers*

There are two major untapped opportunities for creating centers of foreign language/culture knowledge and resources: expanding "One-Stop" partnerships and working with the immigrant/heritage community centers.

"One-Stops" are federally-funded offices managed by local Ohio Department of Jobs and Family Services branches that collect information from people seeking work, provide employee information to potential employers, and provide training to employers and employees. These One-Stops are already work-oriented and may be better equipped than many other organizations (including schools) to see foreign language ability as a value-adding skill.

Immigrant and heritage communities throughout Ohio construct community centers where people with a similar ethnicity can come together for worship, social support, and often, ESL classes. Created as places where immigrants and their descendants can come and feel comfortable in their shared backgrounds, these community centers can also be loci for foreign language instruction. Outside of the community center, many immigrants are sparsely located, living amongst everyone else. Inside these community centers, however, American foreign language learners can find a conveniently-located environment in which their target language is the lingua franca, and the target culture shapes behavior expectations. In addition to being a location for immigrants to learn how to get along in the US, these community centers can become places for Americans to learn how to get along with people from outside the US. Community centers can become publishing houses of target language media and teaching materials, schools for teaching traditional culture (i.e., cooking, traditional arts), and even easy ways to market goods and services to a particular niche market (i.e., halal meats for Muslims).

## Collaboration

The greatest opportunity facing Ohioans may be creating greater collaboration between groups involved in cross-cultural interaction. Many organizations are engaging non-native-English-speaking communities at home and abroad, but many of them are doing so alone. The more collaboration and interaction that these organizations have, the more likely it is that they will be able to share resources and knowledge. Some examples include:

- Non-profit involvement in foreign language education: organizations can provide extra-curricular programs that integrate classroom learning and the real world
- Many countries around the world are promoting their language in response to the expansion of English – the government agencies around the world responsible for this promotion have funds and expertise that can be used to promote learning of their language here in the US.
- Service organizations like Rotary Club and the Lion's Club can help by networking people in similar endeavors.
- The Ohio Department of Tourism is next door to the International Trade Division (both of which are in the Department of Development), making increased cooperation logistically simple.
- Partnerships between business and education, e.g., Battelle's support for The Metro High School, a STEM (science, technology, engineering, and math) focused high school. Businesses that believe foreign language skill is only valuable in conjunction with technical skill can create scholarships for students who major in a technical skill and double major or minor in a foreign language
- Sister city relationships – many of which already exist – can be enhanced by creating more educational and business exchanges.

Educating the public about the utility of foreign language ability may be the grandest form of collaboration yet to happen. Through public education and increased opportunities for cross-cultural interaction and learning, the general public will come to expect foreign language education, rather than begrudge it. Around the world, people study English because they know they can have a better life if they master it. High English proficiency means a good job with good pay – high foreign language proficiency in the US should mean the same thing.

### *Threats*

A significant barrier to achieving widespread and high levels of foreign language ability in Ohio is the fact that foreign language ability is often not materially rewarded by employers. Given two candidates with similar resumes, if one speaks a foreign language and the other does not, the foreign language speaker *may* have an edge in getting hired, but is not likely to be paid more if hired. In many organizations, holders of licenses such as the CPA, CFA, etc, are given raises in return for the added value their knowledge brings to the organization; foreign language skill has no such reward. Without such a reward, there is less incentive to put in the kind of time and energy that is required to master a foreign language.

A related problem is that many organizations settle for less-than-appropriate levels of proficiency – including schools. Without a standard means of assessing professional-level foreign language proficiency, employers have become accustomed to "flying blind," as far as foreign language skills are concerned. Coupled with Ohio's growing economy, it appears to many as if "good enough is good enough." Because Ohio is internationally competitive today, too many Ohioans assume that whatever is working today, will work tomorrow, as well. In this atmosphere, it becomes difficult to convince leaders, students and parents that foreign language ability will be one of the differentiating factors between successful states and unsuccessful states in the 21st century.

**A Report by the Ohio Foreign Language Roadmap Design Teams**

| Domestic Language Roadmap Team | International Language Roadmap Team |
| --- | --- |
| **Laurice Baddour** | **Diane Birckbichler** |
| CulturHable | The Ohio State University |
| **Diane Ging** | **Sharlene Chesnes** |
| Columbus City Schools | InterChez Logistics |
| **Julia Hinten** | **Christopher Farrar** |
| Ohio Department of Development | Percipia |
| **Benito Lucio** | **Roberta Ford** |
| Ohio Department of Jobs & Family Services | US Department of Commerce |
| **Jane McGrew** | **Phil Hayden** |
| Community Refugee & Immigration Services | Hayden Environmental |
| **Mariangee Merino** | **Julia Hinten** |
| US Bank | Ohio Department of Development |
| **Bruno Romero** | **Kimberly Kirkendall** |
| Ohio Supreme Court | China Source Link |
| **Lisa Stokesbury** | **Robert Maynard** |
| VocaLink | Tappan Woods |
| **Mahdi Taakilo** | **Erik Meyer** |
| SomaliLink | Liebert |
| **Ryan Wertz** | **Dixon Miller** |
| Ohio Department of Education | Porter, Wright, Morris & Arthur |
| **Mindy Wright** | **Amelia Rodriguez** |
| The Ohio State University | VocaLink |
| | **Deborah Robinson** |
| | Ohio Department of Education |

Ohio, long a melting pot, has also long been a bastion of conservatism. For many in Ohio, English is the only language they have ever heard, and will ever hear, even though their soybeans or dairy cattle are being exported all over the world. Fear of losing American/English culture to foreign influences – especially Latino culture – and the recognition that the rest of the world is learning English has contributed to the impression in Ohio that English must be the only language used in achieving economic security.

The final major threat – also an opportunity – is competition for resources with mathematics and science education. During the Cold War, mathematics, science and foreign language education were heralded as the path to besting the Russians. Increased spending on mathematics and science education sent men to the moon and pay-per-view to satellites. The key now is to bundle foreign language and technical education *together*. Rather than competing for resources, these two important learning areas should be working to make it possible for American students to learn them together – learning technical skills in foreign languages and learning foreign languages by engaging in technical activities in the classroom.

## APPENDIX A: OHIO GOING GLOBAL; CURRENT FOREIGN LANGUAGE NEEDS AND SUPPLY IN OHIO

### 1. International Foreign Language Needs

#### a. Ohio Foreign Trade

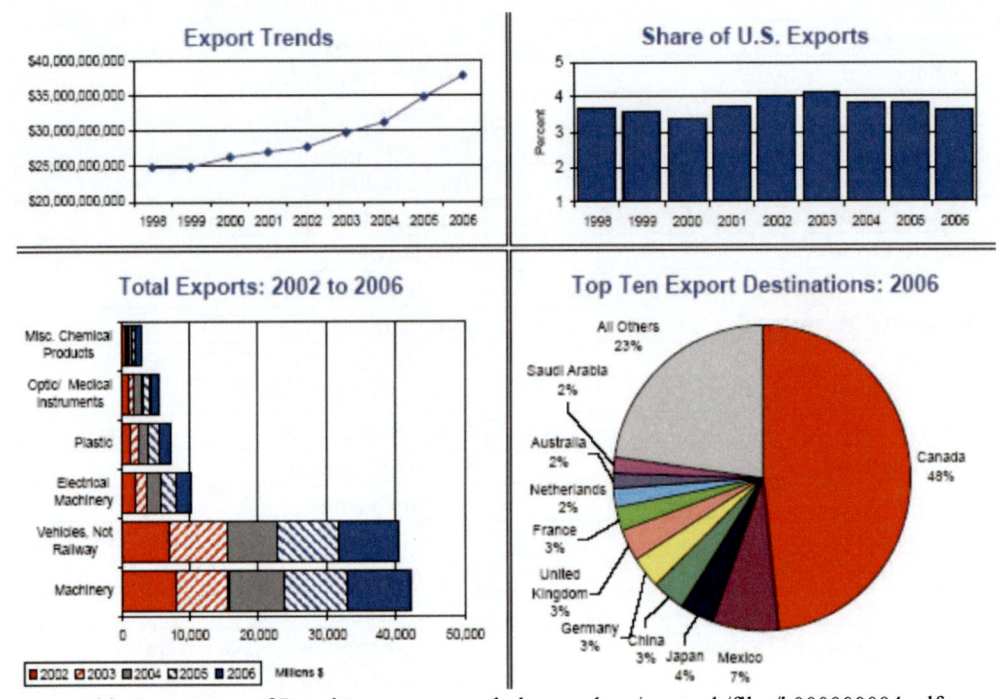

Source: Ohio Department of Development www.odod.state.oh.us/research/files/b000000004.pdf

Ohio Merchandise Exports Snapshot

**Q: How many Ohio jobs rely on export trade?**

- In 2003, export-supported jobs linked to manufacturing accounted for an estimated 6.1 % of Ohio's total private-sector employment (**tied for the seventh among the 50 states**)
- 20.6 % of all manufacturing workers in Ohio depended on exports for their jobs.
- A total of 11,114 companies exported from Ohio locations in 2005, down from 13,048 in 2004. Of these, 89% were small and medium-sized enterprises (SMEs), with fewer than 500 employees.
- 118,700 non-manufacturing jobs in Ohio were supported by manufactured exports in 2003.

From: International Trade Administration, www.export.gov/fta/peru/**ohio**.pdf, http://www.ita.doc.gov/td/industry/otea/state_reports/ohio.html

**Q: What Industries Lead Ohio Exports?**

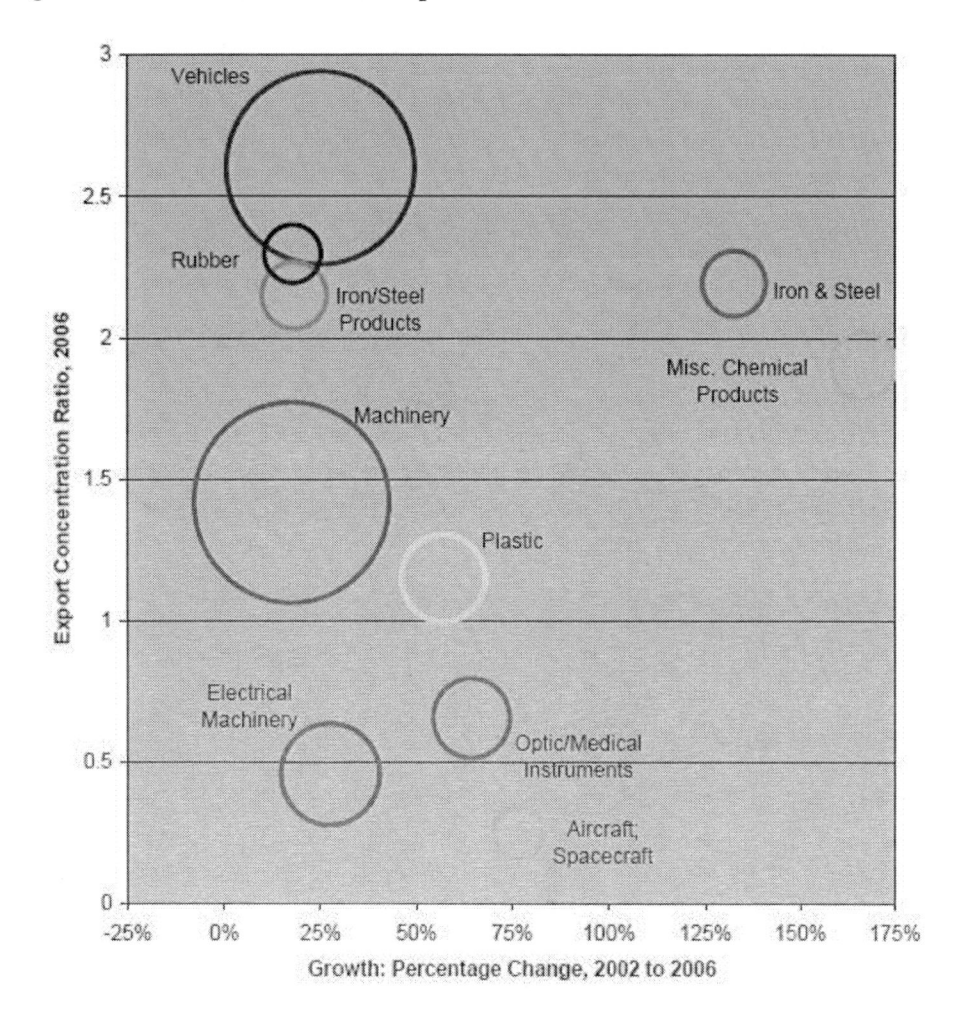

From: Ohio Department of Development, www.odod.state.oh.us/research/ FILES/B000000004.pdf

**Q: Ohio agriculture is big business – how international is it?**
$1.5 billion in agricultural exports in 2005, **13th in nation**
From: USDA www.fas.usda.gov/info/factsheets/WTO/states/oh.pdf
Top 5 Ohio Agricultural Exports

1. Soybeans and soybean products (**#6 in US**)
2. Feed grains and products
3. Wheat and products
4. vegetables
5. poultry and products

From: USDA www.fas.usda.gov/info/factsheets/WTO/states/oh.pdf
and http://www.ers.usda.gov/StateFacts/OH.HTM

**Q: What countries are becoming more important for Ohio exports?**
Between 2002 and 2006, exports to China went up $793 million, Germany up $650 million, Mexico up $599 million, and Saudi Arabia up $424 million. Exports to Russia grew the fastest over the 2002-2006 period, increasing 456 percent. The state also more than tripled its exports to the United Arab Emirates (exports up 282 percent), and Israel (up 264 percent).
From International Trade Administration: http://ita.doc.gov/td/industry/otea/state_reports/ohio.html

**Q: How many Ohio jobs are being lost to international competition?**

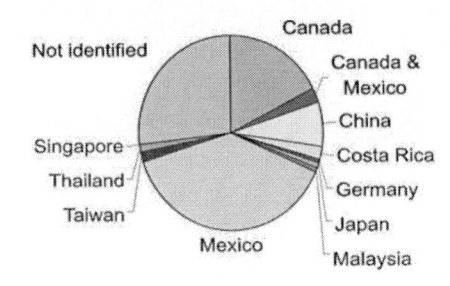

From: Policy Matters Ohio,
http://www.policymattersohio.org/pdf/InternationalTradeJobLossOhio2007.pdf

**Q: What are some Ohio industries seeing exports *decline*?**
(Figures are % change 2005-2006)

10) Aircraft, spacecraft...................................... -4.6%
9) Rubber............................................. -7.6%
8) Engine ignition parts............................-7.9%
7) Passenger vehicle spark/ignition parts.......-10.8%
6) Gas turbines exceeding power 5k KW.......-14.4%
5) Gas turbine parts...............................-25.4%
4) Organic chemicals............................ -28.2%
3) Gear boxes for motor vehicles................-29.7%

2) Passenger vehicle engines >2500cc..........-35.5%
1) Turbojets of thrust >25 KN...................-43%

From: Ohio Department of Development www.odod.state.oh.us/research/files/ b000000004.pdf and US Census Bureau http://www.census.gov/foreign-trade/statistics/ state/data/oh.html

### Q: What kinds of Ohio businesses export services?

- Architectural design (i.e., Jack Rouse Associates of Cincinnati: Projects in China, Hong Kong, Singapore, Guatemala, UAE, Germany)
- Engineering (i.e., Michael Baker Corporation of Cleveland: Projects in Brazil, Russia, Portugal)
- Education (see below)
- Tourism (see below)
- Law firms (i.e., Squire, Sanders & Dempsey of Cleveland: offices worldwide)
- Banking/financial (i.e., National City of Cleveland: International trade services)
- Insurance (i.e., Ohio National Financial Services of Cincinnati: Chile)
- Information services (i.e., Chemical Abstracts Service of Columbus: markets to Japanese, Chinese, Korean readers; OCLC of Columbus: provides library catalog services worldwide)

### Q: What Ohio industries are *not* major exporters?
**Ohio products of 2006 export value less than $5 mil. (out of $37 billion total)**

| Product | 2006 export volume | % change '05–'06 |
|---|---|---|
| Live Animals | $4,753,035 | -10.0 |
| Zinc & Articles Thereof | $4,734,652 | 52.6 |
| Art & Antiques | $4,664,402 | 58.8 |
| Cotton & Yarn, Fabric | $4,179,226 | -17.2 |
| Musical Instruments | $4,162,665 | -22.4 |
| Clocks & Watches | $3,588,154 | 141.5 |
| Lac; Vegetable Sap, Extract | $3,222,867 | 44.4 |
| Headgear | $2,859,446 | 33.9 |
| Live Trees & Plants | $2,639,440 | 4.7 |
| Tin & Articles Thereof | $1,543,483 | -73.3 |
| Fish & Seafood | $1,419,553 | -44.8 |
| Animal Hair & Yarn, Fabric | $915,158 | -31.8 |
| Artificial Flowers, Feathers | $651,743 | 45.7 |
| Other Vegetable Textile Fiber | $516,713 | -4.2 |
| Umbrella, Walking Sticks, etc | $434,838 | 122.1 |
| Cork | $379,190 | -87.5 |
| Straw, Esparto | $316,240 | 32.2 |
| Other Vegetable | $61,714 | -58.9 |
| Furskin & Artificial Fur | $47,199 | -68.8 |
| Tobacco | $10,788 | -90.8 |
| Silk; Silk Yarn, Fabric | $9,479 | 3.0 |

**Q: "We seem to be doing fine with English—why do we need anything else?"**

- Asian English speakers number around 350 million—more than the combined populations of the US, Great Britain and Canada. (From: Newsweek March 7, 2007)

**BUT**

- Trade between countries sharing a common language is 11–170% greater than those without (From: Noguer & Siscart, "Language as a Barrier to International Trade?")
- 20% of SW UK firms in int'l trade felt they had lost business because of language barriers (From: University of Plymouth
- http://www.plymouth.ac.uk/pages/view.asp?page=10312)
- Unless your product/service is vastly superior to all others, businesspeople prefer to do business with native speakers of their own native language
- Even if you do get the contract, who has the power in the relationship, the side that is bilingual or the side that can only speak English?

## b. Foreign Investment in Ohio

**Q: How does Ohio stack up in attracting foreign investment?**

Foreign Direct Investment Rankings by Employment

Most states that score well are on the East Coast, because most FDI comes from Europe and Canada. In 1996, Europe accounted for two-thirds of all FDI in the US, with Asia accounting for less than 15 percent. European companies have invested in East Coast states in part because of their proximity to their corporate headquarters, and because of the access to densely populated markets.

| Rank | State | Score | Rank | State | Score |
|------|-------|-------|------|-------|-------|
| 1 | Hawaii | 8.8% | 11 | Kentucky | 4.8% |
| 2 | South Carolina | 6.7% | 12 | Virginia | 4.4% |
| 3 | North Carolina | 6.2% | 13 | New York | 4.3% |
| 4 | Massachusetts | 5.4% | 14 | Delaware | 4.3% |
| 5 | New Jersey | 5.3% | 15 | Indiana | 4.2% |
| 6 | Georgia | 5.2% | 16 | Pennsylvania | 4.2% |
| 7 | Connecticut | 5.1% | **17** | **Ohio** | **4.2%** |
| 8 | Tennessee | 5.1% | 18 | Rhode Island | 4.1% |
| 9 | New Hampshire | 5.1% | 19 | Illinois | 4.0% |
| 10 | Maine | 4.8% | 20 | California | 3.8% |

From: Progressive Policy Institute,
http://www.neweconomyindex.org/states/1999/part2_page2.html

## Q: Firms from what countries employ Ohioans?

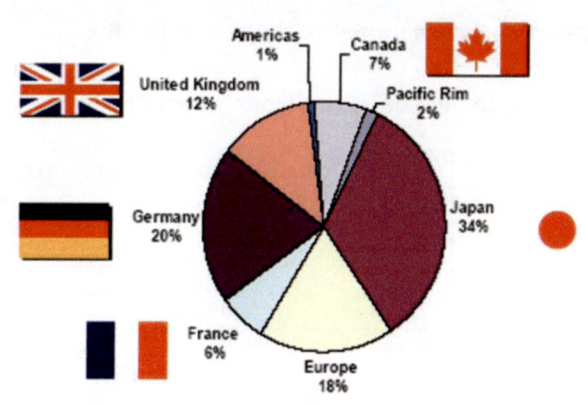

From: http://www.odod.state.oh.us/research/files/b300000000.pdf

International Investment in Ohio (% Employment in State by Country)

## Q: Are foreign companies evenly spread across Ohio?

### by Ohio County

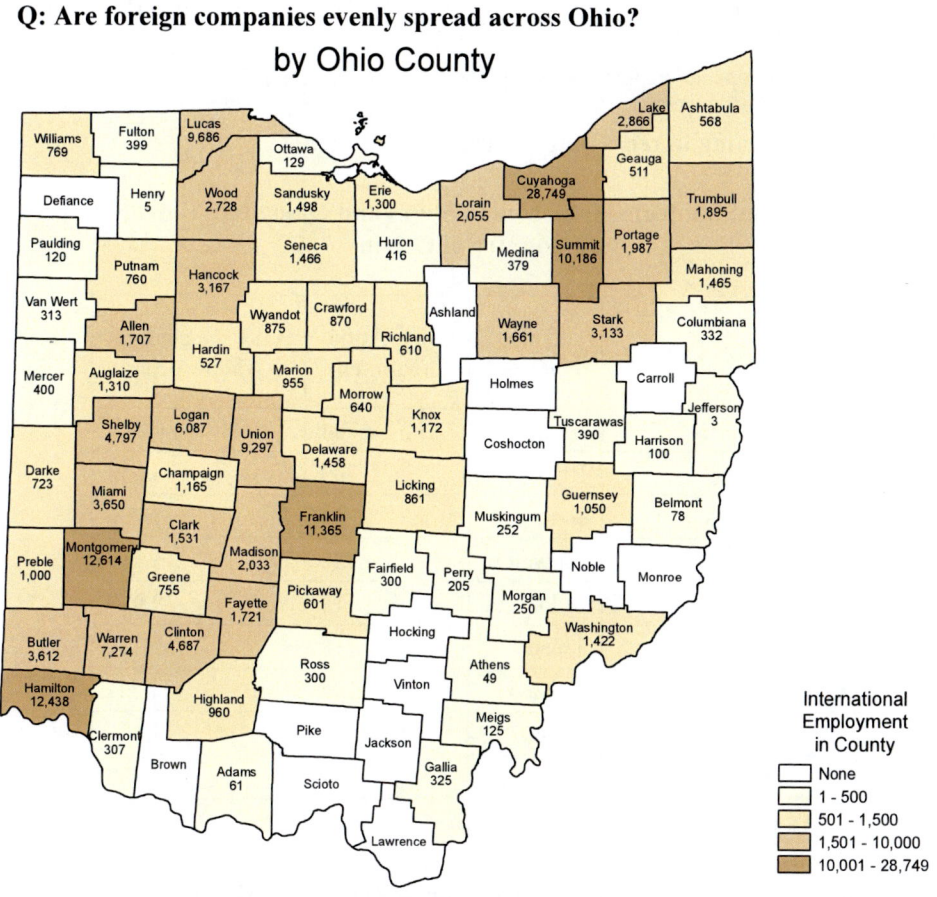

From: http://www.odod.state.oh.us/research/files/b300000000.pdf

Employment in International Operations by Ohio County

## c. International Education

**Q: How does attracting international students benefit Ohio?**

### Economic Impact on States from International Students

| Rank | State | Int'l students 2005/06 | Total contribution 2005/06 |
|---|---|---|---|
| 1 | California | 75,386 | $2,088,377,335.81 |
| 2 | New York | 64,285 | 1,786,324,403.24 |
| 3 | Texas | 46,871 | 891,384,368.48 |
| 4 | Massachusetts | 28,009 | 868,983,709.68 |
| 5 | Florida | 26,059 | 625,041,599.79 |
| 6 | Illinois | 25,114 | 623,538,808.78 |
| 7 | Pennsylvania | 22,419 | 611,293,806.25 |
| 8 | Michigan | 20,826 | 438,531,001.38 |
| 9 | **Ohio** | **18,000** | **424,164,103.77** |
| 10 | New Jersey | 12,781 | 349,341,084.44 |

Adapted from: IIE http://opendoors.iienetwork.org/page/95193/

**Q: How is OSU doing in recruiting international students?**

### International Students in the United States and Ohio State University by Country of Origin

| Rank | US Overall | Ohio State | OSU Au06 enrollment | OSU % change Au05–Au06 |
|---|---|---|---|---|
| 1 | India | PRC | 784 | -0.8% |
| 2 | PRC | ROK | 709 | -6.0% |
| 3 | ROK | India | 503 | -4.7% |
| 4 | Japan | Taiwan | 228 | -5.4% |
| 5 | Canada | Indonesia | 118 | -28.9% |
| 6 | Taiwan | Japan | 118 | -11.9% |
| 7 | Mexico | Canada | 107 | 11.5% |
| 8 | Turkey | Turkey | 105 | -5.4% |
| 9 | Germany | Malaysia | 52 | -23.5% |
| 10 | Thailand | Germany | 41 | -6.8% |

From: International Student Organization http://www.isoa.org/newsletter_february2006.aspx,
Ohio State University Registrar, http://www.ureg.ohio-state.edu/ourweb/srs/srscontent/AU06/
AU06Report.pdf

**Q: Who is setting up international branch campuses to attract overseas students *overseas*?**

As they consider new overseas projects, American colleges face stiff competition from their counterparts in other developed countries, especially Britain and Australia. While there are no reliable figures comparing the numbers of overseas campuses, Australia's institutions appear to be extraordinarily aggressive in planting their flag in other countries: all but one of the 39 government-approved universities in Australia have established overseas degree programs or branch campuses.

From: The Chronicle of Higher Education, www.bus.wisc.edu/insite/events/seminars/documents/HotNewExport_HigherEducation.pdf

Number of Ohio Colleges/Universities found to have overseas degree programs or international branch campuses for foreign students: 0

From: Google search

## 2. Domestic Foreign Language Needs

### a. Immigrant Populations

**Q: How many Ohioans were born overseas?**

#### Ohio Immigrants as Percentage of Population (2003)

| | Foreign Born | | | | | |
|---|---|---|---|---|---|---|
| | Total | | Naturalized U.S. Citizen | | Not a U.S. Citizen | |
| Total pop. in Ohio | Number | Percent | Number | Percent | Number | Percent |
| 11,134,720 | 376,640 | 3% | 181,905 | 48% | 194,730 | 52% |

Adapted from US Census Bureau
http://www.census.gov/population/socdemo/foreign/ST023/tab1-16a.xls

**Q: Where do Ohio's immigrants come from? (2000)**

#### Top 10 Countries of Origin of Immigrants Intending to Live in Ohio 2000

| Country | 1999 | 2000 | % Change |
|---|---|---|---|
| India | 614 | 804 | 31% |
| China | 474 | 712 | 50% |
| Russia | 459 | 516 | 12% |
| Ukraine | 309 | 417 | 35% |
| Romania | 312 | 375 | 20% |
| Canada | 231 | 360 | 56% |
| Mexico | 269 | 345 | 28% |
| United Kingdom | 159 | 285 | 79% |
| Philippines | 210 | 281 | 34% |

Adapted from RAND Florida http://fl.rand.org/stats/popdemo/immmetroST.html

## Q: Where are Ohio's various immigrant populations concentrated?

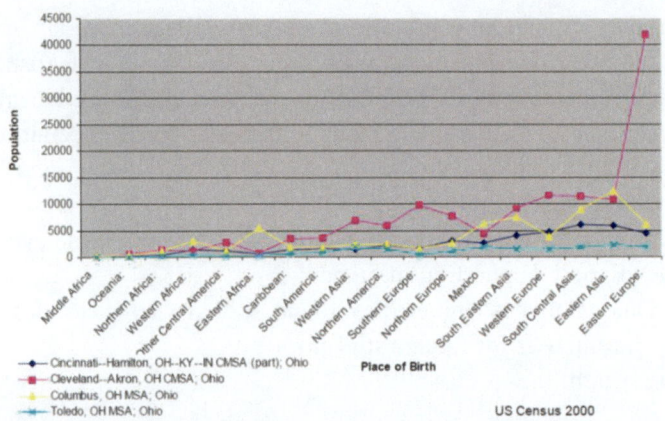

From: The Ohio State University Ohio Agricultural Research and Development Center,
www.farmtomarkets.com/marketinfo/Organic%20OH%20Proud%20Foods.pdf

Ohio Immigrant Population by Metropolitan Area and Region of Birth (2000)

## Q: Does Ohio have refugee populations that may need additional support?

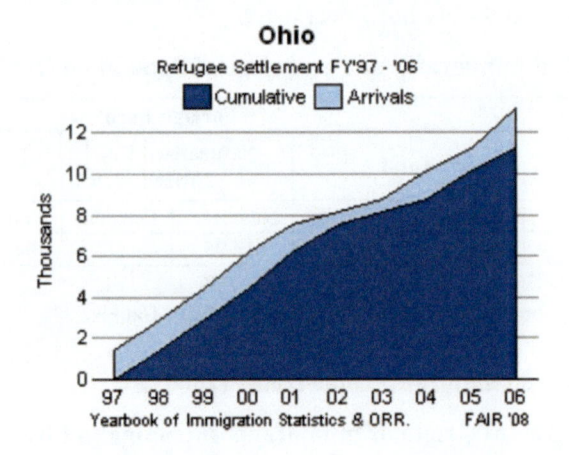

From: Federation for American Immigration Reform
http://www.fairus.org/site/PageServer?pagename=research_researchab92

Ohio Refugee Settlement FY '97–'06

## Country of Origin of Top 5 Refugee Groups Initially Arriving in Ohio in 2004

| Rank | Country of Origin | Number |
|------|-------------------|--------|
| 1 | Somalia | 814 |
| 2 | Liberia | 139 |
| 3 | Ethiopia | 90 |
| 4 | "USSR" | 85 |
| 5 | Burma | 43 |

Adapted from: US HHS http://www.acf.hhs.gov/programs/orr/data/fy2004RA.htm

**Q: What languages are spoken in Ohio?**

### Ohio Speakers of Foreign Languages 2000

| | |
|---|---|
| Spanish | 213,145 |
| German | 72,570 |
| French | 44,395 |
| Italian | 27,695 |
| Arabic | 22,645 |
| Chinese | 21,590 |
| Polish | 16,460 |
| Pennsylvania Dutch | 16,350 |
| Russian | 16,030 |
| Greek | 13,655 |

From: US Census Bureau http://www.fairus.org/site/PageServer?pagename=research_researchab92

**Q: How many potential FL speakers are not in the statistics?**

The Federation for American Immigration Reform estimates that Ohio illegal alien population as of 2005 is about 74,000 persons. Citizenship and Immigration Services (the former INS) estimated in February 2003 that the resident illegal population in Ohio was 40,000 as of January 2000, while the Pew Hispanic Center estimates the illegal alien population of the state at 75,000 to 150,000 as of 2005.

From: http://www.fairus.org/site/PageServer?pagename=research_researchab92

### b. Language Needs in Ohio Public Services

**Q: How does language affect the LEP (Limited English Proficiency) patient healthcare experience?**

Several studies of patients with language barriers who visited an urban hospital emergency department found these patients to be less satisfied with their care, less willing to return to that facility, and less likely to be given a follow-up appointment compared to those without language barriers. Others have found that non-English speakers are less likely to have a usual source of care13 or receive preventive care such as mammography and pap smear tests. From: The Access Project http://www.accessproject.org/adobe/what_a_difference_an_ interpreter_can_make.pdf

Some hospitals use family members or even janitors to translate, which brings up problems of expertise, embarrassment, incomplete translations, and interpretations that are adjusted for cultural mores.

From: CyraCom "Increasing Diversity: Issues and Opportunities with Providing Health Care" June 2006

Many residents also agreed that cross-cultural issues
often resulted in negative consequences including:

• longer office visits (43%)
• patient non-adherence (21%)
• delays in obtaining consent (19%)

From: CyraCom "Increasing Diversity: Issues and Opportunities with Providing Health Care" June 2006

### Language & Quality of Service in Franklin County Health Care

The single largest cause of delays in the past five years is the language barrier presented by the growing number of Somalians, Hispanics, Russian-speaking people, and Asians immigrating to the area. Legally, interviewees said, they must hire interpreters when seeing non-English-speaking patients. Family members or friends of the patient cannot be relied upon for accurate translations. It takes time, resources, and money to do this, and the effect causes delays elsewhere throughout the system that serves the under and uninsured. In addition, of course, the financial hardship is great for providers. There were no funding sources that compensate for the time lost or the money needed to pay interpreters as of this writing.

From: Report to Access HealthColumbus: Improving Access to Primary Care in Franklin County www.accesshealthcolumbus.org/word_doc/**Murray_final_report**.pdf

### Q: What is the level of need for FL speakers in Ohio healthcare?

Midwest Shows Greatest Increase in Healthcare Language Needs

In 2006, the Midwest overtook the South in its percentage growth of languages needed in its hospitals and healthcare facilities, jumping 15 percent in just one year.

From: CyraCom Language Index 2007

Greater Cincinnati hospitals have 2100 patient calls interpreted per quarter. From: Greater Cincinnati Health Council LEP task force http://www.gchc.org/LEPTaskForce /tabid/120/Default.aspx

### Q: How many LEP Medicaid patients did Ohio hospitals serve in 2006 and what were the top languages?

### Total—51,087
### Top Ten Languages Represented by Ohio Medicaid Recipients

| Rank | Language | Medicaid Enrollment |
|------|----------|---------------------|
| 1 | SPANISH | 25,621 |
| 2 | SOMALI (SOMALIA) | 10,360 |
| 3 | ARABIC (MIDDLE EAST) | 3,485 |
| 4 | SPANISH/ENGLISH BILINGUAL | 2,546 |
| 5 | RUSSIAN (RUSSIA) | 1,449 |
| 6 | VIETNAMESE (VIETNAM) | 954 |
| 7 | UKRANIAN (UKRANE) | 879 |
| 8 | MANDARIN (CHINA-SIMPLIFIED) | 857 |
| 9 | FRENCH (FRANCE) | 480 |
| 10 | KHMER (CAMBODIAN) | 411 |

**Q: How qualified are our hospital interpreters?**

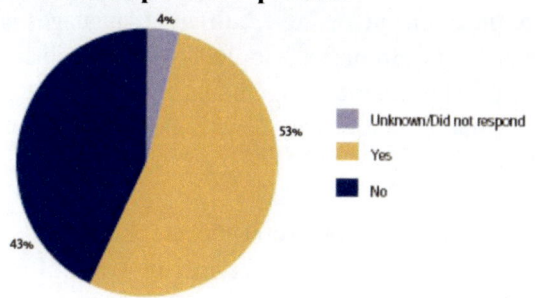

From: Hospitals, Language and Culture: A Snapshot of the Nation
www.jointcommission.org/NR/rdonlyres/E64E5E89-5734-4D1D-BB4DC4ACD4BF8BD3/0/
hlc_paper.pdf
Proportion of Hospital Interpreters/Bilingual Staff Whose Target Language Competency Is Assessed
(Nationally)

**Q: How does Ohio fulfill its healthcare interpretation needs?**

**Resources Available to Hospitals for Providing Language Services by Hospital (%)**

| Census Region | Staff inter-preters | Freelance Interpr-eters | Interpre-tation Agencies | Bilingual Clinical staff | Bilingual nonclinical staff | Community language bank | Tele-phone |
|---|---|---|---|---|---|---|---|
| Northeast | 69 | 62 | 73 | 93 | 85 | 14 | 95 |
| South | 73 | 64 | 61 | 86 | 80 | 19 | 85 |
| **Midwest** | **55** | **66** | **68** | **66** | **53** | **18** | **93** |
| West | 82 | 58 | 63 | 93 | 89 | 20 | 93 |

From: Health Research & Educational Trust "Hospital Language Services For Patients with Limited
English Proficiency"
http://www.hret.org/hret/languageservices/content/languageservicesfr.pdf

**Q: What immigrant populations are likely to need government services?**

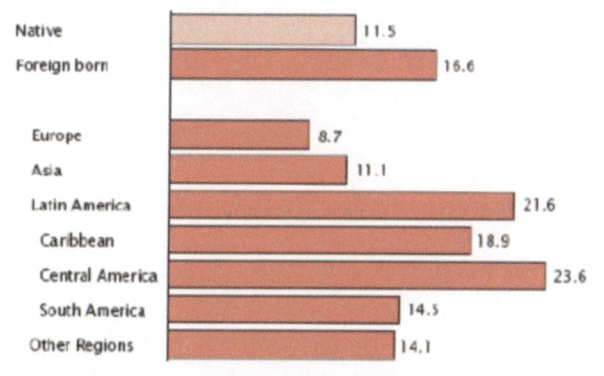

[1]Each bar represents the percent of individuals, who were born in the specified area,
who were living in poverty.
Source: U.S. Census Bureau, Current Population Survey, 2003 Annual Social and
Economic Supplement.

From: US Census Bureau www.census.gov/prod/2004pubs/p20-551.pdf
National Statistics for People Living Below the Poverty Level by Region of Birth 2002 (%)

### Q: How much interpretation happens in Ohio courts?

At least 18,465 interpretations involving 57 different languages were performed in Ohio courts during a 12 month period from 2003 to 2004. After English, the top five languages used in Ohio courts are Spanish, American Sign Language, Somali, Russian and Arabic.

From: The Supreme Court of Ohio www.sconet.state.oh.us/publications/interpreter_ services/interpreter_use_report.pdf

### Q: How much does Ohio court interpretation cost the state?

Ohio courts spent $55,000 on interpreter services in 1998. In contrast, the same courts reported spending roughly $982,000 on interpreters in 2003.

### Q: And how qualified are Ohio's court interpreters?

- Thirty percent of Ohio interpreters have not been trained in interpreter services
- An additional 23 percent of Ohio interpreters have received less than 40 hours of interpreter-related training
- Thirty-two percent of Ohio interpreters have five or fewer years of experience.

From: The Supreme Court of Ohio www.sconet.state.oh.us/publications/interpreter_ services/interpreter_use_report.pdf

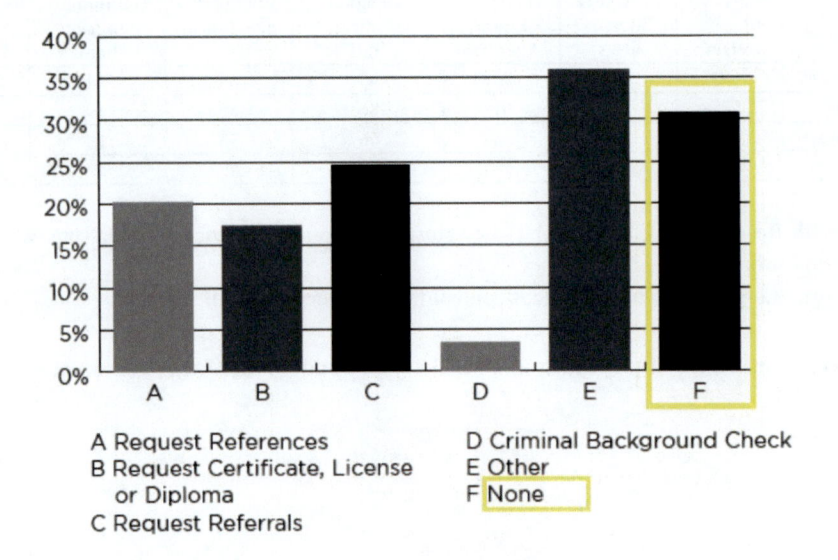

A Request References
B Request Certificate, License or Diploma
C Request Referrals
D Criminal Background Check
E Other
F None

From: The Supreme Court of Ohio
www.sconet.state.oh.us/publications/interpreter_services/interpreter_use_report.pdf

Methods for Qualifying Interpreters in Use in Ohio Courts

**Q: How many K-12 LEP students do Ohio public schools serve?**

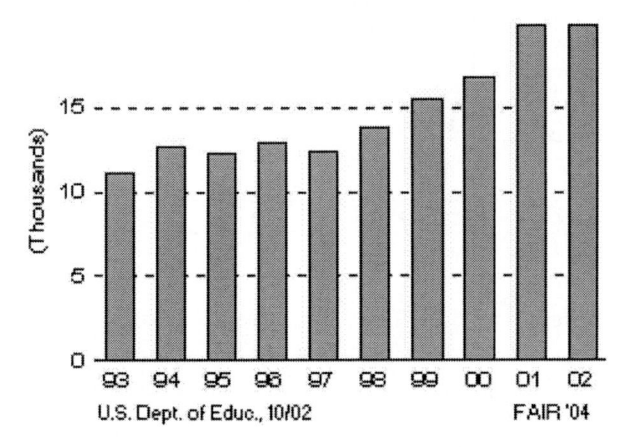

### Ohio LEP/ELL Enrollment K-12
#### School Years '92-'93 to '01-'02

From: http://www.fairus.org/site/PageServer?pagename=research_researchab92

**Q: What languages do Ohio's LEP students speak?**

Ohio's 29,000 LEP students represent more than 100 native/home languages. The top 13 language groups are Spanish, Somali, Arabic, German (mostly Amish), Ukrainian, Japanese, Lao, Vietnamese, Korean, Russian, Serbo-Croatian, Cantonese/Chinese and Albanian

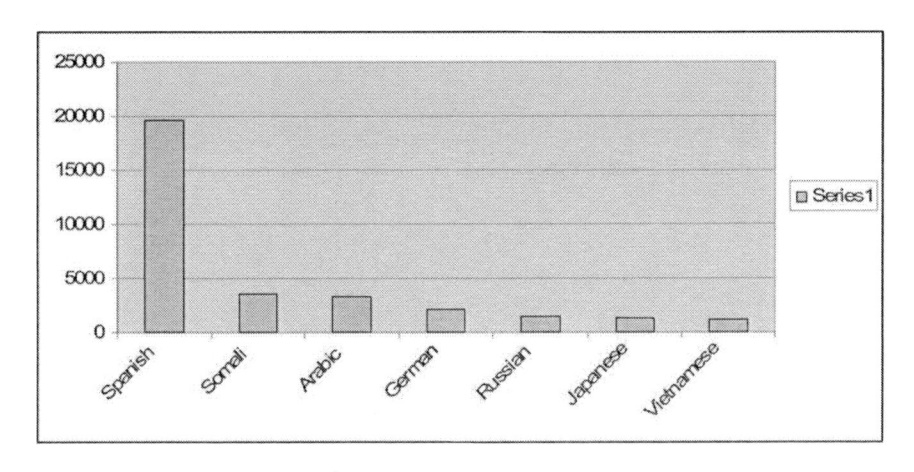

More than 1,100 German-speaking Amish students were enrolled in Holmes County schools 2003–2004.

From: Ohio Department of Education, http://www.ode.state.oh.us/GD/Templates/Pages/
ODE/ODEDetail.aspx?page=3&TopicRelationID=1239&ContentID=1809&Content=27572,
Ohio Foreign Language Advisory Council April 18, 2007 meeting data

Languages Spoken by ≥ 1000 K-12 Heritage and/or LEP students

## c. Ohio's Domestic Business Foreign Language needs

**Q: In what occupations would Americans interact most with foreign-born employees?**

| Occupation type | % of Native-born labor working in this field | % of Foreign-born labor working in this field |
|---|---|---|
| Management, professional | 36.4% | 26.4 |
| Service | 15.4% | 22.5 |
| Natural resources, construction | 10.0% | 16.5 |
| Production, transportation | 11.9% | 16.7 |

Source: Bureau of Labor Statistics

**Q: How much of the labor force in the Heartland is foreign born?**

By region, the foreign born comprised 24.0 percent of the total labor force in the West, 17.9 percent in the Northeast, and 13.5 percent in the South. By comparison, only 7.3 percent of the total labor force in the Midwest was foreign born.

From: Bureau of Labor Statistics www.bls.gov/news.release/pdf/forbrn.pdf

Between 1996 and 2003 **immigrants accounted for 84 percent of labor-force growth** in eastern North Central states (Indiana, Illinois, Michigan, Ohio, and Wisconsin) and 47 percent in eastern South Central states (Alabama, Kentucky, Mississippi, and Tennessee).

From: Economic Report of the President, in Immigration Policy in Focus, http://www.ailf.org/ipc/economicsofnecessity.asp

**Q: How many foreign employees working in Ohio are not immigrants, and are even more likely to prefer speaking in their native language than immigrants?**

- 7,499 foreign workers due to intra-company transfers
- 1,233 foreign workers related to NAFTA
- 68,886 foreigners for other business

From: NAR research, www.**real**tor.org/Research.nsf/files/IntlBusOH.pdf/$FILE/ IntlBusOH.pdf

**Q: What Jobs do Ohio's Immigrants have?**

### Top 10 Occupations of Immigrants Intending to Live in Ohio 2000

| Category | 1999 | 2000 | % Change |
|---|---|---|---|
| Homemakers | 880 | 908 | 3% |
| Private household service | 168 | 345 | 105% |
| Unemployed | 189 | 283 | 50% |
| Executive, administrative, managerial | 236 | 268 | 14% |
| Administrative support, including clerical | 147 | 226 | 54% |
| Marketing and sales personnel | 115 | 156 | 36% |
| Handlers, equipment cleaners, helpers and lab | 53 | 119 | 125% |
| Computer, mathematical, O.R. scientists | 38 | 112 | 195% |

Adapted from RAND Florida, http://fl.rand.org/stats/popdemo/immmetroST.html

**Q: I've heard that America's food production industry would collapse without migrant labor. How many migrant workers did Ohio have at last count?**

15,782 (primarily Latino)

From: Ohio Department of Jobs and Family Services, http://jfs.ohio.gov/agriculture/Census.PDF

**Q: I've heard that many construction workers are foreign – is this true for Ohio?**

| | % of Construction Workers by Place of Birth | | | | |
| | Immigrant Construction Worker's Place of Birth | | | | |
| State | Americas | Asia | Europe | Other | NativeBorn |
|---|---|---|---|---|---|
| California | 31.36 | 3.95 | 2.19 | 0.33 | 62.17 |
| Nevada | 33.3 | 1.48 | 1.7 | 0.2 | 63.32 |
| Texas | 33.33 | 1.07 | 0.73 | 0.1 | 64.77 |
| District of Columbia | 31.25 | 1.35 | 1.59 | 0.52 | 65.3 |
| Arizona | 31.55 | 0.59 | 1.77 | 0.51 | 65.58 |
| Ohio | 2.45 | 0.44 | 1.89 | 0 | 95.22 |
| Indiana | 4.15 | 0.27 | 0.35 | 0 | 95.23 |
| US Total | 15.41% | 1.46% | 2.28% | 0.21% | 80.63% |
| US Total | 1,925,017 | 182,359 | 284,766 | 26,709 | 10,070,000 |

From: National Association of Home Builders, http://www.nahb.org/generic.aspx?genericContentID=49216

**Q: What might LEP consumers want or need to buy?**

"Due to language, cultural and institutional adjustments, homeownership among recent immigrants lags behind that of native-born Americans and the population as a whole."

From: NAR research www.**real**tor.org/Research.nsf/files/IntlBusOH.pdf/$FILE/IntlBusOH.pdf

Traditionally, Ohio is not a goat state, and goats raised in Ohio are mostly for the local 4-H markets. However, with the tremendous influx of immigration and increasing health consciousness of the population, there seems to be a large market for goat meat in Ohio.

From: Ohio Cooperative Development Center, http://ocdc.osu.edu/pdf/anal_proposal.pdf

It is estimated that Columbus Somalis consume the meat from about 14,000 goats each year.

From: University of Minnesota http://ageconsearch.umn.edu/feed/rss_2.0/123456789/8376

Said a Bangladeshi restaurant owner, "halal meat is a big issue… Right now we buy from Sysco, but who knows if they are keeping our laws. Maybe if the farmer is close we would also like to buy eggplant, cauliflower, green peppers, onions, garlic, carrots, mint, and cilantro."

From: The Ohio State University Ohio Agricultural Research and Development Center, www.farmtomarkets.com/marketinfo/Organic%20OH%20Proud%20Foods.pdf

JPMorgan Chase's banking products make it difficult for low-income customers to take the first step into financial security. JPMorgan Chase's savings accounts are subject to service fees of $4 per month unless the minimum daily balance exceeds $300. A full-time janitor cleaning JPMorgan Chase's McCoy Corporate Center in Polaris earning $1,200 per month would likely see their savings eroded for months before earning a positive return.

Access to banking services remains a challenge to many immigrant customers. JPMorgan Chase tends not to have translation at bank branches in Columbus's growing Latino and Somali communities, despite these communities accounting for the city's largest foreign-born ethnic groups.

From: PR Newswire, http://news.corporate.findlaw.com/prnewswire/20070412/12apr20071335.html

Traditional [home] finance options contradict the values and teachings of Islam. Once developed, compliant programs must receive endorsement from a board of Islamic Scholars, known as Sharia Board. Both American and Islamic approvals are difficult to receive and have forced most Muslims to wait.

Because of this lack of available solutions, demand has been pent up and could cause undue pressure on Ohio Muslims to conform to our system and values. This would be a mistake and show a lack of understanding of both culture and foundation for Muslim beliefs.

From: The Columbus Board of Realtors, http://www.columbusrealtors.com/15839.cfm

**Q: How many foreign tourists does Ohio get, and where do they come from?**
97,282 foreigners came to Ohio for vacation in 2004

From: NAR research www.realtor.org/Research.nsf/files/IntlBusOH.pdf/$FILEIntlBus OH.pdf

Ohio's biggest markets (besides Canada) are:

1. German speaking Europeans (Germany, Austria, Switzerland)
2. Japanese (we don't market to them) and
3. English speaking Europeans (UK and Ireland).

French, Italians, Spanish, etc. are very small volume to the Great Lakes.

From: personal communication with Ohio Division of Travel and Tourism 5/1/07

**Q: What travelers are coming to the states that Ohio is not currently capturing?**

**Top 10 Nationalities of Foreign Travelers to the US, 2005 (non-English-speaking countries not in above Ohio list highlighted)**

| Rank | Residence | Arrivals | Rank | Residence | Arrivals |
|------|-----------|----------|------|-----------|----------|
| 1. | Canada | 14,865,000 | 6 | France | 878,648 |
| 2 | Mexico | 12,858,000 | 7 | South Korea | 705,093 |
| 3 | United Kingdom | 4,344,957 | 8 | Australia | 581,773 |
| 4 | Japan | 3,883,906 | 9 | Italy | 545,546 |
| 5 | Germany | 1,415,530 | 10 | Brazil | 485,373 |

From: Office of Travel and Tourism Industries/International Trade Administration on
http://www.infoplease.com/ipa/A0778214.html

Total travel to the US from non-Visa Waiver countries was up five percent in 2006, outperforming total travel from the 27 Visa Waiver countries, which was down three percent. Travelers from non-Visa Waiver countries are required to obtain U.S. visas before entry into the U.S, therefore it is notable that growth occurred in a segment for which there is a perceived "barrier to entry."

## China

Arrivals from the People's Republic of China totaled a **record 320,000**, up 19 percent from 2005. A vast majority of Chinese travel is business travel.

The Department of Commerce is working to explore a commercial agreement with the Chinese government to open market access and permit group leisure travel to the U.S. and the related marketing of U.S. destinations and firms.

## Spain

Spanish visitation to the U.S. totaled a **record 424,000** in 2006, up 10 percent from 2005. The 2006 growth rate was slightly less than the 16 percent rate in 2005. Unlike other Western European countries in 2006, visitation from Spain grew by double digits during the second, third and fourth quarters, up 17 percent, 12 percent and 17 percent, respectively.

From: International Trade Administration, http://tinet.ita.doc.gov/view/a-2006-400/index.html

## 3. Current Ohio Foreign Language Learning Capacity

**Q: Is Ohio ahead, keeping up with, or behind national FL enrollments?**

**Change in Ohio, National Public Secondary School Foreign Language Enrollments, 1994–2000**

| | FL Enrollments | | | PSS Enrollments | | | FL as % of PSS | | |
|---|---|---|---|---|---|---|---|---|---|
| | 1994 | 2000 | % Change | 1994 | 2000 | % Change | 1994 | 2000 | % Change |
| OH | 274,815 | 287,541 | 4.43% | 818,739 | 822,440 | 0.45% | 33.57% | 34.96% | 1.40% |
| US | | | 12.01% | | | 9.16% | | | 1.06% |

From: ACTFL http://www.actfl.org/files/public/Enroll2000.pdf

## Regional Comparison of 2002 Undergraduate Enrollments in Sixteen Leading Languages

| Language | Northeast | Midwest | South Atlantic | South Central | Rocky Mountain | Pacific Coast | National (Total) |
|---|---|---|---|---|---|---|---|
| Spanish | 143,587 | 157,214 | 167,090 | 87,819 | 58,837 | 121,770 | 736,317 |
| Percentage of national | 19.5 | 21.4 | 22.7 | 11.9 | 8.0 | 16.5 | 100.0 |
| French | 46,540 | 44,680 | 48,065 | 19,088 | 11,452 | 27,549 | 197,374 |
| Percentage of national | 23.6 | 22.6 | 24.4 | 9.7 | 5.8 | 14.0 | 100.0 |
| German | 16,580 | 27,456 | 18,870 | 6,702 | 6,634 | 12,055 | 88,297 |
| Percentage of national | 18.8 | 31.1 | 21.4 | 7.6 | 7.5 | 13.7 | 100.0 |
| Italian | 26,192 | 10,459 | 9,350 | 2,813 | 3,101 | 10,937 | 62,852 |
| Percentage of national | 41.7 | 16.6 | 14.9 | 4.5 | 4.9 | 17.4 | 100.0 |
| American Sign Language | 8,818 | 11,613 | 7,744 | 4,989 | 6,882 | 20,614 | 60,660 |
| Percentage of national | 14.5 | 19.1 | 12.8 | 8.2 | 11.3 | 34.0 | 100.0 |
| Japanese | 9,132 | 9,980 | 6,582 | 2,320 | 4,023 | 19,271 | 51,308 |
| Percentage of national | 17.8 | 19.5 | 12.8 | 4.5 | 7.8 | 37.6 | 100.0 |
| Chinese | 8,822 | 5,166 | 4,228 | 1,431 | 1,933 | 11,639 | 33,219 |
| Percentage of national | 26.6 | 15.6 | 12.7 | 4.3 | 5.8 | 35.0 | 100.0 |
| Latin | 6,127 | 7,197 | 7,200 | 3,736 | 1,688 | 2,848 | 28,796 |
| Percentage of national | 21.3 | 25.0 | 25.0 | 13.0 | 5.9 | 9.9 | 100.0 |
| Russian | 6,034 | 5,198 | 4,159 | 1,442 | 2,289 | 4,029 | 23,151 |
| Percentage of national | 26.1 | 22.5 | 18.0 | 6.2 | 9.9 | 17.4 | 100.0 |
| Greek | 2,111 | 4,128 | 3,750 | 1,982 | 780 | 1,592 | 14,343 |
| Percentage of national | 14.7 | 28.8 | 26.1 | 13.8 | 5.4 | 11.1 | 100.0 |
| Biblical Hebrew | 5,732 | 1,242 | 1,132 | 357 | 135 | 452 | 9,050 |
| Percentage of national | 63.3 | 13.7 | 12.5 | 3.9 | 1.5 | 5.0 | 100.0 |
| Arabic | 2,184 | 2,219 | 2,246 | 652 | 692 | 2,060 | 10,053 |
| Percentage of national | 21.7 | 22.1 | 22.3 | 6.5 | 6.9 | 20.5 | 100.0 |
| Modern Hebrew | 4,091 | 1,491 | 1,207 | 280 | 339 | 793 | 8,201 |
| Percentage of national | 49.9 | 18.2 | 14.7 | 3.4 | 4.1 | 9.7 | 100.0 |
| Portuguese | 2,202 | 1,250 | 1,886 | 516 | 1,244 | 800 | 7,898 |
| Percentage of national | 27.9 | 15.8 | 23.9 | 6.5 | 15.8 | 10.1 | 100.0 |
| Korean | 1,147 | 592 | 393 | 152 | 323 | 2,493 | 5,100 |
| Percentage of national | 22.5 | 11.6 | 7.7 | 3.0 | 6.3 | 48.9 | 100.0 |
| Vietnamese | 113 | 45 | 97 | 117 | 36 | 1,780 | 2,188 |
| Percentage of national | 5.2 | 2.1 | 4.4 | 5.3 | 1.6 | 81.4 | 100.0 |

From: Modern Language Association http://www.mla.org/pdf/enrollments.pdf

## Q: What languages see the highest enrollments in Ohio public schools?
### Top 10 Ohio Foreign Language Enrollments grades K-12 '05–06

| National Rank | Ohio Rank | Language | Ohio Enrollment |
|---|---|---|---|
| 1 | 1 | Spanish | 214624 |
| 2 | 2 | French | 59403 |
|   | 3 | Foreign Language Exp (middle school) | 21420 |
| 3 | 4 | German | 20282 |
| 7 | 5 | Latin | 10184 |
|   | 6 | Early Learning Spanish (K-8) | 9039 |
|   | 7 | Early Learning French (K-8) | 2809 |
|   | 8 | AP Spanish Language | 1859 |
| 4 | 9 | Italian | 1350 |
| 5 | 10 | Japanese | 1184 |

From: Ohio Department of Education, Modern Language Association 2002 enrollment survey
   http://www.adfl.org/resources/enrollments.pdf

**Q: How many students are Ohio schools sending abroad, where they might achieve advanced FL skills?. . .**

### American Students Engaged in Study Abroad by State 2004/2005

|  | State | Total |
|---|---|---|
| 1 | Total | 205983 |
| 2 | California | 19408 |
| 3 | New York | 15933 |
| 4 | Pennsylvania | 13378 |
| 5 | Texas | 9866 |
| 6 | Massachusetts | 9186 |
| 7 | **Ohio** | **8948** |
| 8 | Minnesota | 8182 |
| 9 | Michigan | 7774 |
| 10 | Virginia | 7561 |

Adapted from: http://opendoors.iienetwork.org/?p=89228

**Q: ...And where do American students tend to go abroad?**

|  | Rank Destination | 2003/04 | 2004/05 | 2004/05 % of All Study Abroad | 2004/05 % Change |
|---|---|---|---|---|---|
|  | TOTAL | 191,321 | 205,983 |  | 7.7 |
| 1 | **United Kingdom** | **32,237** | **32,071** | **15.6** | **-0.5** |
| 2 | Italy | 21,922 | 24,858 | 12.1 | 13.4 |
| 3 | Spain | 20,080 | 20,806 | 10.1 | 3.6 |
| 4 | France | 13,718 | 15,374 | 7.5 | 12.1 |
| 5 | **Australia** | **11,418** | **10,813** | **5.2** | **-5.3** |
| 6 | Mexico | 9,293 | 9,244 | 4.5 | -0.5 |
| 7 | Germany | 5,985 | 6,557 | 3.2 | 9.6 |
| 8 | China | 4,737 | 6,389 | 3.1 | 34.9 |
| 9 | **Ireland** | **5,198** | **5,083** | **2.5** | **-2.2** |
| 10 | Costa Rica | 4,510 | 4,887 | 2.4 | 8.4 |

From: IIE http://opendoors.iienetwork.org/?p=89212

**Q: Do Ohio State students learn foreign languages where *they* study abroad?**

Highlighting added to show known non-language programs; about 20 students in China were on language programs in that year.

### Ohio State Study Abroad Destinations, SY2005–2006

| Rank | Destination | Student # | % of total |
|---|---|---|---|
| 1 | England | 295 | 17% |
| 2 | France | 131 | 7% |
| 3 | Brazil | 131 | 7% |
| 4 | Italy | 97 | 5% |
| 5 | Germany | 95 | 5% |
| 6 | Australia | 80 | 4% |
| 7 | China | 71 | 4% |
| 8 | Spain | 62 | 3% |
| 9 | South Africa | 49 | 3% |
| 10 | Hong Kong | 49 | 3% |

From: Ohio State University Office of International Education

## APPENDIX B: SURVEY OF OHIOANS' VIEWS ABOUT FOREIGN LANGUAGE & CULTURE

Scripps Survey Research Center
Ohio University
August 2007
For 2007 U.S. Language Summit
Ohio Roadmap in Language Excellence

### Summary of Findings

**\*Respondents believe knowledge of foreign language and cultures of other countries helps national security and international trade.**

- Two-thirds of respondents believe foreign language instruction should begin in grade school.
- 49.3% of respondents believe foreign language should be a requirement for high school graduation.
- 34.7% of respondents believe foreign language should be a requirement for graduation from state universities.
- Residents of suburbs are more likely to favor foreign language than those who live in big cities, small cities and rural areas.
- People over 55 are more supportive of foreign language instruction than younger people.
- People less than 35 years of age more likely to support requiring foreign language for high school and university graduation.
- 55.3 percent of respondents believe businesses should provide opportunities for employees to learn foreign language.

A telephone survey of 521 randomly selected Ohio adults found that they believe knowledge of foreign languages and foreign cultures is important to the state and that more needs to be done in public education. The survey was conducted from August 21 to August 29 by the Scripps Survey Research Center Ohio University. It was funded by the 2007 U.S. Language Summit Ohio Roadmap for Language Excellence.

Table 1 shows that more than three-fourths of the respondents believe that knowledge of foreign language will increase national security, help international trade, help us understand better the culture of other countries and help us to serve people better who have limited language skills.

However, less than half the respondents believe knowledge of foreign languages will bring more jobs to Ohio, but 84.3 percent think ability to speak another language will make a person more employable.

Table 2 indicates that respondents feel knowledge of other cultures will have similar effects. It will help increase international trade and national security and help bring about world peace. However, as with knowledge of foreign languages, less than half believe that knowledge of other countries' cultures will bring more jobs to Ohio.

**Table 1. Effects of Knowledge of Foreign Language**

| | |
|---|---|
| Knowledge of foreign languages helps national security | 86.0% |
| Knowledge of foreign languages helps international trade | 91.9% |
| Knowledge of foreign languages increases our ability to serve people in Ohio with limited language skills | 79.1% |
| Knowledge of foreign languages will help us better understand cultures of other countries | 86.6% |
| Knowledge of foreign languages will bring more jobs to Ohio | 47.4% |

Yet combing these two sets of questions, we have a clear indication that knowledge of foreign languages and other countries' cultures will improve the quality of life in Ohio.

**Table 2. Effects of Knowledge of Other Cultures**

| | |
|---|---|
| Knowledge of other countries' cultures will help increase international trade | 73.5% |
| Knowledge of other countries' cultures will help bring about world peace | 63.0% |
| Knowledge of other countries' cultures will increase our national security | 71.0% |
| Knowledge of other countries' cultures will bring more jobs to Ohio | 41.5% |

The vast majority of respondents feel that the study of foreign languages should begin in grade school, as Table 3 shows. Respondents were also asked if foreign language should be required for graduation from high school, as math and science are by law in Ohio. Only 49.3 percent thought so, but 82 percent of parents with children at home said they wanted their child to learn a foreign language. Only 34.7 percent thought ability to communicate in a foreign language should be required in Ohio's state universities. Given the support of foreign language study indicated by the responses shown in Table 1, these figures are surprisingly low. Of those who said foreign language should be required in high school, 5.8 percent said one year, 51 percent said two years, 14.8 percent aid three years and 25.3 percent said four years should be required.

**Table 3. Needed Education in Foreign Languages**

| | |
|---|---|
| Students should begin learning languages in | |
| Grade School | 67.0% |
| Junior High School | 16.5% |
| High School | 9.2% |
| Foreign languages should be required for graduation from high school | 49.3% |
| Being able to communicate in a foreign language should be a graduation requirement at stateb universities | 34.7% |

We also asked respondents whether they thought foreign languages in high school were more important, as important or less important than athletics, art and after-school activities. Table 4 shows that more people consider foreign languages more important than athletics, art and after-school activities than considered foreign languages less important. However, the most frequent response was that foreign languages are equally important.

**Table 4. Importance of Foreign Languages in High School**

|  | More Important | As Important | Less Important | Don't Know |
|---|---|---|---|---|
| Compared to athletics, foreign languages are | 32.2% | 42.4% | 18.4% | 6.9% |
| Compared to art, foreign languages are | 24.4% | 49.7% | 19.2% | 6.7% |
| Compared to after-school programs, foreign languages are | 27.1% | 45.3% | 27.6 % | |

We asked respondents what languages Ohioans should be able to speak. Not surprisingly, as Table 5 shows, Spanish was the No. 1 choice by a wide margin. Japanese was a clear second choice at 44.7 percent, followed by Arabic and Chinese at 30.9 percent and 30.7 percent respectively. It should be noted that the first three are from three different regions— Western Europe, Far East and Middle East.

**Table 5. What Languages Ohioans Should Be Able to Speak**

| Spanish | 72.0% | Hindu | 20.5% |
|---|---|---|---|
| Japanese | 44.7% | French | 19.6% |
| Arabic | 30.9% | Farsi | 14.0% |
| Chinese | 30.7% | Somali | 16.9% |
| Russian | 23.2% | Swahili | 11.3% |

Table 6 show responses to several other matters related to the importance of foreign languages. On foreign trade, 39.5 percent of our respondents said it is very important to Ohio's economy, and 46.6 percent said it is somewhat important. Nearly 30 percent said it is very important for immigrants to remain fluent in their first language, and 44.3 percent said it is somewhat important. We also found that 55.3 percent of our respondents thought businesses should provide opportunities for their employees to learn foreign languages and 51.1 percent thought businesses should provide opportunities for their employees to learn about cultures of other countries.

### Demographic Factors

All groups in Ohio do not see these issues the same way. Women are slightly more favorably inclined toward foreign language than men are, and the more educated people also are more favorably inclined toward foreign languages. However, the differences are small for the most part.

**Table 6. Attitudes on Other Issues**

|  | Very Important | Somewhat Important | Not Important | Don't Know |
|---|---|---|---|---|
| How important is foreign trade to Ohio's economy? | 39.5% | 46.4% | 8.1% | 6.0% |
| How important is it for Ohioans to be able to communicate in another language? | 30.3% | 45.3% | 21.9% | 2.5% |
| How important is it for immigrants to maintain fluency in their first language? | 29.4% | 44.3% | 19.2% | 7.1% |

Differences related to where people live and their age are more substantial. Table 7 shows how those in big cities, small cities, suburbs and rural areas feel about the effect of knowledge of foreign language. As Table 7 shows, those who live in suburbs are more likely to see positive effects of knowledge of language and those who live in small cities are less likely to see positive effects.

**Table 7. Effects of Knowledge of Foreign Languages by Where Respondent Lives**

| Knowledge of foreign language... | Large City | Small City | Suburb | Rural Area |
|---|---|---|---|---|
| Helps national security | 83.7% | 80.2% | 90.7% | 87.7% |
| Helps international trade | 93.5% | 85.5% | 96.0% | 94.1% |
| Increases ability to serve people with limited English skills | 78.3% | 77.1% | 86.8% | 76.2% |
| Helps us better understand other cultures | 85.9% | 83.9% | 90.1% | 81.5% |
| Will bring more jobs to Ohio | 50.0% | 42.7% | 53.6% | 44.6% |
| N | 92 | 131 | 151 | 130 |

Older people are more likely to see positive effects of knowledge than younger people, as Table 8 shows. For four of the five items, the figure for those more than 55 years of age is higher than that for either those 18 to 34 years old or those 35 to 54 years old. Those who are 18 to 34 years old are more likely to see positive effects than those 35 to 54 years old. The most striking difference is on whether knowledge of foreign language will bring more jobs to Ohio where 53.6 percent of those over 55 agree and only 42.7 percent of those between 35 and 54 agree.

Table 9 shows that those who live in suburbs are more likely to favor starting foreign languages in grade school and more likely to favor making foreign language a high school graduation requirement, yet oddly enough they are less likely than those who live in big cities or small cities to favor foreign language s a graduation requirement for the state universities. The greater support for foreign language in grade schools and foreign language in suburbs may to some extent reflect awareness of the greater resources that suburban schools tend to have.

**Table 8. Effects of Knowledge of Foreign Languages by Age**

|  | 18-34 | 35-54 | More Than 55 |
|---|---|---|---|
| Knowledge of foreign language: |  |  |  |
|   Helps national security | 83.7% | 80.2% | 90.7% |
|   Helps international trade | 93.5% | 85.9% | 90.7% |
|   Increases ability to serve people with limited English Skills | 78.3% | 77.1% | 86.8% |
| Helps us better understand other cultures | 85.9% | 83.9% | 90.1% |
| Will bring more jobs to Ohio | 50.0% | 42.7% | 53.6% |
| **N** | **72** | **219** | **215** |

**Table 9. Needed Education in Foreign Language by Where Respondent Lives**

|  | Large City | Small City | Suburb | Rural Area |
|---|---|---|---|---|
| Students should begin study of foreign language: |  |  |  |  |
|   In grade school | 67.4% | 63.4% | 73.5% | 69.2% |
|   In junior high school | 18.5% | 18.3% | 16.6% | 14.6% |
|   In high school | 9.8% | 14.5% | 5.3% | 6.9% |
| Foreign language should be required for graduation from high school | 47.8% | 51.9% | 58.4% | 42.3% |
| Being able to communicate in foreign language should be graduation requirement in state universities | 39.1% | 40.3% | 35.1% | 28.5% |
| N | 92 | 131 | 151 | 130 |

There is not much difference between age groups in support of starting foreign language in grade school, as Table 10 shows. However, those under 35 are more likely to favor foreign language as a high school graduation requirement for both high school and state universities.

**Table 10. Needed Education in Foreign Language by Age**

|  | 18–34 | 35–54 | More Than 55 |
|---|---|---|---|
| Students should begin study of foreign language |  |  |  |
|   In grade school | 66.7% | 68.5% | 67.4% |
|   In junior high school | 19.4% | 19.2% | 14.0% |
|   In high school | 9.7% | 8.7% | 9.2% |
| Foreign language should be required for graduation | 56.9% | 54.3% | 42.4% |
| from high school |  |  |  |
| Being able to communicate in foreign language | 41.7% | 32.4% | 35.3% |
| should be graduation requirement in state universities |  |  |  |
| N | 72 | 219 | 215 |

*Technical Appendix*

    Survey was conducted by telephone from the Scripps Survey Research Center at Ohio University. Interviewing was done by student workers who were trained in interviewing. Respondents were picked by random-digit dialing using a sample provided by Survey Sampling International. Interviewing began August 21 and ended August 29. Interviews were conducted between 6 and 9:30 p.m. Sunday through Thursday.

## APPENDIX C: OHIO CITIES WITH SISTER CITIES ABROAD

| Community | Sister City |
| --- | --- |
| Akron | Chemnitz, Sachsen, Germany |
| Akron | Kiryat Ekron, Israel |
| Ashtabula | Bardejov, Presovsky, Slovakia |
| Blue Ash | Ilmenav, Thueringen, Germany |
| Centerville | Bad Zwischenahn, Niedersachsen, Germany |
| Centerville | Waterloo, Ontario, Canada |
| Chillicothe | Cordoba, Veracruz-Llave, Mexico |
| Cincinnati | Gifu, Japan |
| Cincinnati | Harare, Harare, Zimbabwe |
| Cincinnati | Kharkiv, Kharkivs'ka (Kharkiv), Ukraine |
| Cincinnati | Liuzhou, Guangxi, China |
| Cincinnati | Munich, Bayern, Germany |
| Cincinnati | Nancy, Lorraine, France |
| Cincinnati | Taipei-Hsien, Taiwan, Other |
| Cleveland | Conakry, Guinea |
| Cleveland | Ibadan, Nigeria |
| Cleveland | Segundo Montes, Morazan, El Salvador |
| Cleveland | Volgograd, Volgogradskaya, Russia |
| Cleveland | Taipei Municipality, Taiwan, Other |
| Cleveland | Holon, Israel |
| Cleveland | Lima, Amazonas, Peru |
| Cleveland | Heidenheim, Hessen, Germany |
| Cleveland | Miskolc, Borsod-Abauj-Zemplen, Hungary |
| Cleveland | West Mayo, Mayo, Ireland |
| Cleveland | Bahir Dar, Ethiopia |
| Cleveland | Fieri, Albania |
| Cleveland | Alexandria, Egypt |
| Cleveland | Klaipeda, Klaipedos Rajonas, Lithuania |
| Cleveland | Bangalore, India |
| Cleveland | Brasov, Brasov, Romania |
| Cleveland | Bratislava, Bratislavsky, Slovakia |
| Cleveland | Cleveland County, England, UK |
| Cleveland | Gdansk, Pomorskie, Poland |
| Cleveland | Ljubljana, Cankova-Tisina, Slovenia |
| Colerain Township | Munich-Obergiesing/Fasangarten, Bayern, Germany |
| Columbus | Dresden, Sachsen, Germany |
| Columbus | Genoa, Liguria, Italy |
| Columbus | Hefei, China |
| Columbus | Herzliya, Israel |
| Columbus | Odense, Fyn, Denmark |
| Columbus | Seville, Andalucia, Spain |
| Columbus | Tainan City, Taiwan, Other |
| Dayton | Augsburg, Bayern, Germany |
| Dayton | Holon, Israel |
| Dayton | Monrovia, Bomi, Liberia |

**(Continued)**

| Community | Sister City |
|---|---|
| Dayton | Oiso, Japan |
| Dayton | Sarajevo, Bosnia and Herzegovina |
| Hamilton | Hamilton, Scotland, UK |
| Huber Heights | Rheinsberg, Brandenburg, Germany |
| Huber Heights | Dover, England, UK |
| Kent | Dudince, Banskobystricky, Slovakia |
| Kettering | Kettering, England, UK |
| Kettering | Steyr, Oberoesterreich, Austria |
| Lima | Harima, Japan |
| Montgomery | Neuilly-Plaisance, Ile-de-France, France |
| Oakwood | Le Vesinet, Ile-de-France, France |
| Oakwood | Outremont, Quebec, Canada |
| Oberlin | Ile-Ife, Nigeria |
| Portsmouth | Gorby, England, UK |
| Portsmouth | Orizaba, Mexico |
| Portsmouth | Zittau, Sachsen, Germany |
| Springfield | Kragujevac, Serbia |
| Springfield | Berwick, Australia |
| Springfield | Lutherstadt Wittenberg, Sachsen-Anhalt, Germany |
| Springfield | Pitesti, Arges, Romania |
| St. Mary's | Awaji City, Japan |
| St. Mary's | Lienen, Nordrhein-Westfalen, Germany |
| Toledo | Londrina, Parana, Brazil |
| Toledo | Qinhuangdao, Hebei, China |
| Toledo | Szeged, Csongrad, Hungary |
| Toledo | Toledo, Castilla-La Mancha, Spain |
| Toledo | Toyohashi, Aichi, Japan |
| Toledo | Tanga, Tanzania |
| Toledo | Delmenhorst, Niedersachsen, Germany |
| Toledo | Poznan, Poland |
| Vandalia | Lichtenfels, Bayern, Germany |
| Vandalia | Prestwick, Scotland, UK |
| Wapakoneta | Lengerich, Nordrhein-Westfalen, Germany |

From: Sister Cities International, http://www.sister-cities.org/icrc/directory/usa/OH

# END NOTES

[1] Youngstown, Ohio, for one, has an active and locally-integrated sister city program.
[2] A list of Ohio's sister cities can be found in Appendix C
[3] Much of the German investment in Ohio was in Daimler-Chrysler. Now that Chrysler has been sold to Cerberus, it is unclear what the current value of German investment in Ohio is.

In: Building Strategic Language Ability Programs
Editor: Joshua R. Weston

ISBN: 978-1-60741-127-7
© 2010 Nova Science Publishers, Inc.

*Chapter 3*

# STATEMENT OF TERRI E. GIVENS, UNIVERSITY OF TEXAS AT AUSTIN, BEFORE THE HOUSE ARMED SERVICES COMMITTEE SUBCOMMITTEE ON OVERSIGHT AND INVESTIGATIONS

## I. INTRODUCTION AND BACKGROUND

Mr. Chairman and members of this distinguished committee, thank you for the opportunity to speak with you regarding the University of Texas at Austin's Language Flagships and the Texas Language Roadmap.

***Open Doors* 2007**
***Report on International Educational Exchange***

**Institutions by Total Number of Study Abroad Students: Top 10 Doctoral/Research Institutions, 2005/06**

| Rank | Institution | City | State | Students |
|------|------------|------|-------|----------|
| 1 | New York University | New York | NY | 2,809 |
| 2 | Michigan State University | East Lansing | MI | 2,558 |
| 3 | University of Texas–Austin | Austin | TX | 2,244 |
| 4 | Penn State University–University Park | University | Park PA | 2,168 |
| 5 | University of Illinois–Urbana-Champaign | Champaign | IL | 1,988 |
| 6 | University of Minnesota–Twin Cities | Minneapolis | MN | 1,981 |
| 7 | University of California–Los Angeles | Los Angeles | CA | 1,966 |
| 8 | University of Florida | Gainesville | FL | 1,926 |
| 9 | University of Georgia | Athens GA | | 1,916 |
| 10 | Ohio State University–Main Campus | Columbus | OH | 1,858 |

The following document provides an overview of study abroad and language enrollment at the University of Texas at Austin. I also provide information on funding for study abroad programs. Section III provides detailed information on the two Language Flagship programs at the University and Section IV provides information on the Texas Language Roadmap.

The University of Texas at Austin is one of the leaders in education abroad and language education in the United States. We have consistently ranked in the top 5 over the last few years in numbers of students studying abroad at doctoral/research institutions, and we are currently ranked 3rd as shown in the Open Doors 2005/2006 report:

The university teaches a broad range of languages as shown in the following table:

**Fall 2006 Language Enrollments at the University of Texas at Austin**

| | |
|---|---|
| Spanish | 4442 *(216 are graduate level)* |
| French | 1319 *(94 are graduate level)* |
| German | 801 *(75 are graduate level)* |
| Italian | 580 *(7 are graduate level)* |
| Japanese | 408 *(7 are graduate level)* |
| Chinese | 362 |
| Latin | 352 *(25 are graduate level)* |
| American Sign Language | 290 |
| Russian | 282 *(22 are graduate level)* |
| Arabic | 223 *(36 are graduate level)* |
| Portuguese | 168 *(13 are graduate level)* |
| Ancient Greek | 147 *(50 are graduate level)* |
| Hindi | 135 *(10 are graduate level)* |
| Korean | 109 |
| Persian | 87 *(4 are graduate level)* |
| Hebrew, Modern | 73 *(5 are graduate level)* |
| Urdu | 54 *(5 are graduate level)* |
| Czech | 40 *(2 are graduate level)* |
| Turkish | 38 *(1 is graduate level)* |
| Tamil | 30 *(4 are graduate level)* |
| Vietnamese | 29 |
| Yoruba | 29 |
| Sanskrit | 27 *(5 are graduate level)* |
| Dutch | 13 |
| Danish | 12 |
| Norwegian | 12 |
| Serbo-Croatian | 12 |
| Malayalam | 10 |
| Swedish | 10 |
| Bengali | 8 |
| Polish | 4 |
| Yiddish | 3 |

** The survey measures enrollments, not the number of students studying a language other than English.
Source: Modern Language Association

## II. Financing Study Abroad at the University of Texas at Austin

General Information:

- Because there are no large funding sources, students must gather financial support from various entities to piece together a financial plan.
- Strategic financing (like Gilman and Flagships putting focus on non traditional locations) is not in and of itself enough to change the American student's overwhelming desire to go to Europe and Australia. Much more will have to change on campuses around the US in order to shift the destination trends. Until that time, more American students will be going into great financial debt to study abroad in traditional locations like France, Italy, Spain and the UK.
- In cases where students are selecting to go to non traditional locations and programs the money available becomes more competitive each year, as even those funding sources are limited.
- Funds for middle income students are perhaps the most challenging; no single or collective scholarship initiative is addressing this issue.
- The University is currently in the process of re-evaluating funding for Study Abroad and plans to provide more institutional support in order to reduce the program costs for students

## International Education Fee Scholarship (UT)

Began in 1990.

Student leaders worked with the Texas Legislature to allow students to add a $1-$3 fee to tuition in order to fund study abroad scholarships for undergraduate and graduate students.

As of Fall 2007, UT has awarded over $1,790,000 in financial support to undergraduate and graduate students (grad: $358,083; under: $1,433,406). Serving over 2100 students (grad: 384; under: 1804).

Undergraduate awards range from $1000–$1500 with approximately a 35% award rate. Graduate awards range from $1200–$1500 with less than a 20% award rate.

## Benjamin a Gilman International Scholarship

Began in 2000.

http://www.iie.org/programs/gilman/stats/Annual%20App%20&%20Award%20Stats%2006-07.pdf

Requires Pell grant; very small percentage of our study abroad applicants are Pell granted or Pell eligible

In 2006/2007 they had 2195 applicants and awarded 777 students (35% of applicant pool awarded).

Awards are generally $3000 - $5000 per student.

New Critical Need Language Supplement, $3000 per student.

As of fall 2006, UT has had 45 award recipients for a total of $179,400 (an embarrassing figure when looked at in comparison to other states and institutions of our size and caliber). Every year UT SAO faces a huge challenge of recruiting students for this scholarship. We have been unable to determine why our number of applicants is low given that UT has approximately 7500 students receiving a Pell grant each year.

## Fulbright US Student Program:

Began in 1946.

Awarded approximately six thousand grants in 2007, at a cost of more than $262 million, to U.S. students, teachers, professionals, and scholars to study, teach, lecture, and conduct research in more than 155 countries, and to their foreign counterparts to engage in similar activities in the United States.

The nation's only comprehensive scholarship program for international education.

## Freeman–Asia

Began 2000.

Since the launch of the program in 2000, Freeman-ASIA has supported almost 4,000 U.S. undergraduates with their study abroad plans in East and Southeast Asia. Award amounts range from $3000 - $7000.

## Coop GOES

Began in 2002.

The University Coop (our campus bookstore) has donated funds ranging from $100,000 to $250,000 per year to fund study abroad scholarships for Maymester (short-term faculty led programs) and summer study abroad programs.

2004–2008 Co-op GOES Awards for Maymester courses total $731,000 for 471 undergraduate and graduate students.

Funding for summer courses began in 2005

2005–2008 Co-op GOES Awards for Summer courses total $352,000 for 160 undergraduate and graduate students

## American Airlines

Began in 2006.

American Airlines gives UT three airline tickets per year. (3 awards / possible, 2000 applicants)

## AT&T

Began in 2007

The AT&T scholarship provides $120,000 to students studying abroad over the period of three years. In order for these funds to actually impact a student's financial situation we try to ensure that the minimum award is $2000. If that trend continues, at the end of the contract approximately 60 students will be served.

# III. Language Flagships at the University of Texas at Austin

The University of Texas at Austin has received funding for 2 Language Flagship programs from the National Security Education Program. The Hindi Urdu Flagship currently has 15 students and the Arabic Flagship has 39 students. This program is an important source of funding for our brightest students who have an interest in intensive language study.

## The Hindi Urdu Flagship

The Hindi Urdu Flagship at the University of Texas at Austin is the sole Language Flagship program dedicated to this pair of languages. Building on a long history of teaching South Asian languages and cultures at UT, HUF is responding to a newly-perceived national need to change the paradigm of language learning in the US by developing new pedagogical approaches, a new type of curriculum, and a new focus on the Flagship goal of producing global professionals—graduates whose linguistic skills will make them highly effective in a range of professional capacities.

Hindi and Urdu share a common grammar and basic vocabulary, but are distinct in script, higher vocabulary and cultural orientation; their sibling relationship allows us to teach the two in parallel, a unique feature within the Flagship family of languages. Currently beginning its second year of operation, HUF is showing early success in both main aspects of its operation — (a) providing innovative teaching for students of Hindi-Urdu at UT, and (b) bringing innovative development to the teaching and learning of these languages nationwide. The most significant new emphasis in the Flagship approach is to transcend the traditional 'Language and Literature' context of language study and to develop students' linguistic skills in disciplines and areas directly relevant to their long-term professional ambitions; thus each student will be taken through four years of language training with an appropriately designed curriculum based on compatibility with his or her major, and with close attention being paid to the individual student's development. Our students represent a variety of majors, including Business, Pre-med, Biology, Communication, Electrical Engineering, and various liberal arts fields. Such diversity represents a broad spectrum of linguistic needs that we are addressing through several new approaches, briefly outlined here:

- A focus on *specific themes* in language classes: for example, the second-year syllabus for the current semester includes a focus on Ecology and Environment, building students' familiarity with a technical lexicon closely relevant to the worlds of science, development, and public administration.

- The study of Hindi and Urdu sources as a supplement to existing UT courses such as South Asian anthropology, history and politics; the aim here is to give students the South Asian perspective in these fields through study in the requisite discipline *through the target language.*
- In collaboration with the UT South Asia Institute, we invite distinguished Hindi and Urdu writers and artists to visit UT and work with our students.
- The development of innovative authentic learning and teaching materials, many being designed for self-study through such media as podcasts and web-based video.
- A newly-conceived and carefully planned period of immersion language-study in India, for the third year of a student's program. Based on intensive language training at the long-established American Institute of Indian Studies, the Flagship 'Year in India' will include two specific and unique features: (a) mentorship and teaching of individual students in their major subjects by Indian university faculty (for UT credit); and (b) internships in NGOs and other organizations related to individual students' majors.

The role of a Flagship is not merely to teach its own students, but also to raise the level of language teaching and learning across the board. In a series of workshops held at UT, we have been working towards new ways of training teachers in our languages. This is an especially urgent need for Hindi and Urdu, where much teaching is currently an inadequate combination of mother-tongue knowledge and amateur enthusiasm. We will be expanding our training process with recommendations for curriculum and best practice, and will be making such training available in the vital sector of K-12 in which lie the best possibilities for channeling students towards the advanced study of our languages. Since it is well known that the goal of advanced proficiency in language is best achieved by students who began their studies at a young age, our Flagship teachers have taken part in the development of Hindi Urdu language standards for K-12, and have actively contributed to the Startalk program in teacher-training and in summer-study initiatives.

Although our primary constituency for recruitment to the HUF program has so far been among students with a South Asian heritage, we have also been successful in recruiting students with no South Asian family background – students whose induction into Hindi-Urdu has been triggered by personal interest in South Asia, its cultures and its peoples. We expect to continue to draw on both Heritage and non-Heritage constituencies, and to develop ways of meeting the different learning needs of these two groups while they collaborate and study together as equally valued participants in the Flagship community. Our Flagship students, all very busy, with many irons in the academic fire, show real dedication to their Hindi-Urdu studies as they work towards taking their Hindi Urdu knowledge to the professional level. Here are four examples of our current students:

- One HUF student, a Heritage student majoring in Finance, has recently been accepted into the highly competitive Business Honors Program in UT's McCombs School of Business. He hopes to pursue pre-medicine courses alongside the Finance track and will graduate in 2011 with dual majors in Finance and Asian Studies. After graduation, he will either embark on a career in finance or enter medical school.

- Another HUF student, also a Heritage student, is a Biology major in the College of Natural Sciences. Having recently moved with his family to the US from Nepal, he qualified for UT's TIP Program (Texas Interdisciplinary Plan) that mentors the academic success of 'transitional' students who show exceptional academic promise. This student's professional goals are intensely humanitarian. He will graduate in 2011 with majors in Biology and Asian Studies and will enter medical school with the plan to use his skills in Hindi and Urdu in collaboration with international humanitarian organizations.
- A third HUF student is a non-Heritage student who will graduate with majors in Biology and Asian Studies at the end of her study abroad year in 2010. An exceptional student, her intention has been to become a doctor and work in international health programs, such as 'Doctors Without Borders.' After joining the HUF Program, however, she has become interested in pursuing Hindi-Urdu and South Asia studies at the graduate level in order to become a Hindi specialist.
- A Heritage student who is a Government major in UT's College of Liberal Arts serves as a final example. This student has chosen an Urdu focus in the Flagship Program and will graduate in 2011 with two Liberal Arts majors: Government and Asian Studies. She hopes to pursue graduate school and eventually work in the field of international relations.

We seek to recruit students nationwide, and even at international schools in South Asia that enroll American expatriates; we have already had some success in this endeavor thanks to the support of the University of Texas in providing tuition waivers, i.e., in charging in-state fees to out-of-state students. The success of the program as a truly *national* resource is wholly dependent on such an arrangement. The essential cooperation and support of the university has also been forthcoming in other important ways, for example:

- UT has provided the program with fine office and teaching space in the heart of the campus, close to the Department of Asian Studies, the academic base of HUF's directors and instructors. This space provides an essential center for the program's activities, and helps us to promote the aims of the Flagship in the wider academic community.
- The university authorities have worked closely with the HUF team in finding the most cost-efficient ways of channeling funding to individual students, through detailed caseby- case analysis of students' financial packages.
- The staff of UT's Liberal Arts Instructional Technology Services collaborate closely with HUF in developing innovative teaching materials, allowing the Flagship to play a full part in the development of language-teaching pedagogy in the university while also benefiting from the experience of colleagues in other languages.

As has already been noted, the Hindi Urdu Flagship is contributing to the national Language Flagship's 'Diffusion of Innovation' process by creating and distributing innovative materials for use wherever Hindi-Urdu is taught. The Flagship also values collaborative projects, and has recently won NSEP funding for a new project, 'Language for Health: the Practice of Medicine in Hindi and Urdu,' to be undertaken in collaboration with Columbia University and New York University. This project addresses the urgent need to train medical and healthcare practitioners in Hindi and Urdu so that they can function professionally in South Asian medical contexts both in the US and in South Asia. We expect this collaborative project to be the first of many such, and through work of this kind we shall continue to develop the Language Flagship ideal of producing linguistically sophisticated professionals in many different fields.

All aspects of HUF's activities will be subject to scrutiny through a rigorous peer-review process; the Flagship emphasis on evidence-based learning scrutinizes both the achievement of the student and the efficacy of the teaching program, allowing us to make constant adjustments and improvements to our operation. We are confident that the Hindi Urdu Flagship will each year graduate a group of highly skilled and knowledgeable students who will be able to function in Hindi Urdu in their professional capacities and to make a significant impact on relations between South Asia and the USA. We expect that both employers in the private sector and the government will be competing for these Flagship graduates. The success of our program at undergraduate level encourages us to think of broadening our sphere of activity; at planning sessions in the coming weeks and months we will be evaluating various ideas for new initiatives in the future.

# ARABIC FLAGSHIP PROGRAM

The Arabic Flagship Program (AFP) at the University of Texas at Austin provides training in Arabic language and culture at the undergraduate level. AFP students are given the opportunity to reach Superior level proficiency (Level 3 on the ILR government scale) in Arabic while simultaneously pursuing an undergraduate major of their choice.

The program is unique in several key ways. The first is that our program is embedded within the Department of Middle Eastern Studies, enabling us to offer a very wide range of Arabic language and content courses. Also, the substantive benefits the AFP program has brought to UT in terms of increased faculty, smaller class sizes, increased contact hours for students, benefit all of the students in our program rather than only our own. UT Austin has the largest Arabic faculty in the country, and the close, supportive relationship we enjoy with our Department has benefitted all enormously.

A second factor that makes our program unique is that the majority of our students are non-heritage students. This means that we are able to target and recruit students based on academic talent, language aptitude and commitment rather than the level of language they bring with them. We have also seen an increase in the number of students transferring to UT Austin during their undergraduate degrees in order to be an AFP scholar. Incoming freshmen are applying to our program in greater numbers, in some cases turning down Ivy League offers to join us here.

Another key difference is that students have the opportunity to take content courses in a wide range of subjects, and these are taught in Arabic. Examples of these Arabic content courses include a course on the political system in Lebanon, courses on Arabic Literature, History, and Religions. As our program expands, we expand the variety of courses available to our students. One new innovation is our Language Across the Curriculum courses, where students study in English but are offered an additional one hour where they read authentic texts in Arabic and discuss them using the target language.

## Profile of Our Students

The typical AFP student has already had 1–2 years of Arabic by the time they are accepted into our program. The average GPA is 3.5 or above, and they come from a wide variety of backgrounds and majors. What unites them is an absolute commitment to developing professional level proficiency in Arabic and true talent for learning languages that enables them to keep up with a very challenging program of study. After completion, our students plan work in academia, for the government, in international business, in global advertising, and a range of other fields.

We currently have 39 students in our program, with five of these in Egypt working on their capstone year. Interest is extremely high and we already have applications on file for our next recruitment cycle in January. One reason why recruitment has been so successful is that we select students from inside our wider UT Arabic program, and then, these same students attend classes with the general population. This means they serve as role models for other students, and students often ask, "There is an AFP student in my class and their Arabic is great – how can I get into your program?"

Over the period of their five years in the program, AFP students will move from taking Arabic language courses, where they work on both Modern Standard Arabic as well as specialize in an Arabic dialect, to more advanced dialect work, to content and Media courses taught inArabic. Through their time studying in the Middle East that is part of the program, they build ontheir language skills to add a deep understanding of culture as well. This means that we are able to create the next generation of global language professionals.

## Study Abroad in Alexandria, Egypt

We offer our students two opportunities to study abroad during their time with us through a program in Alexandria Egypt administered by the American Councils for International Education. Alexandria offers a friendly and safe seaside environment where exposure to English is limited, while the University of Alexandria's long established center for Teaching Arabic as a Foreign Language provides the faculty and facilities we need to achieve our aims. The Language Flagship Organization as a whole has invested in building a strong center and upgrading facilities on the ground in Egypt, and we are working hard to build a long-term relationship that will enhance our stateside program.

Our students will spend one full summer at the TAFL Center in Egypt when they reach the Intermediate High level and one full year to make the transition from Advanced to Superior Arabic. This 4 [years at UT] + 1 [year in Alexandria] model enables students to focus on their undergraduate degrees fully while here, meaning that Business and Medical students can be accommodated within it without compromise, and then focus exclusively on Arabic in their capstone year. Feedback from students in Egypt at present indicates that all is going well, with diverse personalized internships and a rigorous academic curriculum in place.

## The Arabic Language Community

On entry to the program, AFP students are assigned a mentor for individual weekly tuition to help them to develop their listening and speaking skills. This increases their exposure to Arabic as it is spoken across the Middle East, and provides an entry into Arab cultures. Our department routinely hosts several Fulbright Teaching Assistants from across the Middle East, and they become active in our program, acting as mentors and participating in classes and events.

During the year, we host a wide range of events, films and speakers so that students are part of a vital and growing community at UT. Some examples from this past year of events were the visit from renowned Lebanese singer, Marcel Khalife, a film series focusing on current cultural issues dominating the Middle East, and a student led Arabic Talent Show. Future plans include the creation of an Arabic living environment, Arabic House, for our students and visiting faculty to take part in, creating a true immersion experience here in Texas.

## Sharing Our Innovations

The Flagship mission is not just to create a small pool of well-trained students, but instead to change the face of language teaching across the country. We are taking the lead in a wide range of projects to provide leadership to the Arabic teaching community. This year, we will be focusing on K-12, Outreach, Testing and Assessment, and upgrading our website to become a valuable resource for learners of Arabic.

We have been chosen for two Diffusion of Innovation Projects this year, and one additional collaborative project. We will be working closely with the University of Michigan as they expand their Arabic materials development and student program, and the University of Oklahoma as they build on their existing program. Within our collaborative project, we are working with the American Council on the Teaching of Foreign Languages (ACTFL) on building consensus on the way oral Arabic skills are tested and how the results are interpreted.

The outcomes of these projects will have a profound impact on the Arabic teaching community at large and we are looking forward to sharing our successes and learning from the successes and experience of others as we go forward.

## Creating the Next Generation of Arabic Educators

A final goal of our program that we have had great success with is the creation of the next generation of Arabic language teachers. We have recruited many of the top graduate students in the country who provide classroom assistance, work on research projects, and take our program forward. Graduate level classes in the Teaching of Arabic as Foreign Language are offered, and our seven Arabic Flagship Graduate Scholars are encouraged to write, research, and share their experiences. This year at the Middle Eastern Studies Association meeting, seven of our current and past Flagship mentors will be presenting papers.

We provide the academic input, the language support, and the practical classroom experience our graduate students need to become successful professionals, and the extra guidance and mentoring they receive here makes places them in high demand.

## The Arabic Flagship Future

The Arabic Flagship program at UT is serving the nation by producing students with a high level of proficiency in Arabic language and culture and teachers who will be at the forefront of teaching Arabic. Continuing the Flagship funding will be essential in enabling UT to continue to fulfill these critical national needs.

# IV. THE TEXAS LANGUAGE ROADMAP

In February 2007, the University of Texas at Austin was selected as one of three institutions around the country to participate in the federally-funded 2007 U.S. Language Summits project. The results of that project are summarized below. In the spring of 2008, Dr. Terri Givens was asked to continue the project, in order to develop an advisory board which would work with the State of Texas to develop the ideas outlined in the Language Summit. We currently have 5 high-profile members of the advisory board, and we are working with the Austin Chamber of Commerce to develop ties to the business community. The main focus of the initiative will be to develop and fund pilot language projects in elementary schools, work towards legislation that would increase requirements for language training, and provide broader funding for K-12 language initiatives.

## TEXAS IN A CHANGING WORLD

- Texas has been ranked the number 1 U.S. exporting state for the past 6 years
- Texas exports 15% of its output, 1 in 4 manufacturing jobs is linked to overseas demand
- Global mergers and acquisitions have resulted in more U.S. companies being owned by foreign parent companies
- Today's workforce in multinational corporations are more involved in multicultural teams around the world (global teams)
- The following are the top ten countries that Texas exports to:

| 1  | Mexico          | *(↑2.2%)  |
|----|-----------------|-----------|
| 2  | Canada          | *(↑6.9%)  |
| 3  | China           | *(↑24.6%) |
| 4  | South Korea     | *(↑4.1%)  |
| 5  | Netherlands     | *(↑19.7%) |
| 6  | Taiwan          | *(↑31%)   |
| 7  | Singapore       | *(↑29.4%) |
| 8  | Brazil          | *(↑22.6%) |
| 9  | Japan           | *(↑24.5%) |
| 10 | United Kingdom  | *(↑12.8%) |

* refers to % change from 2006-2007

One quarter of Texas gross national product is exported to Asia, the fastest growing sector for Texas.

- The Office of the Governor, Economic Development and Tourism (2007) reports that Texas receives 8 million tourists annually, an estimated 4.9 billion into the economy
- The service sector including tourism, healthcare, finance, law and information services have seen increases in its overseas clients.
- Asian populations in Texas operate 78,000 businesses generating 20.6 billion annually

Source: http://www.trade.gov/td/industry/otea/state_reports/texas.html and http://governor.state.tx.us/

## Changes in the Population

- Minority groups such as Hispanics, African Americans and Asian Americans are now in the majority, over half of the state is non-white
- Texas now has the third largest African American and Asian American populations
- The rate of increase of Native Americans, Hawaiian and Pacific Islanders and Alaskan natives is now the 2nd highest in the country

Source: Real Estate Center at Texas A&M University (2007)

## THE DEMAND FOR LANGUAGES OTHER THAN ENGLISH IN TEXAS

### Advanced Language Competency

- English is the primary form of communication in business but other languages like Spanish, French, Chinese and Vietnamese are also commonly used
- There is a lack of Asian language speakers, especially technology-geared languages like Chinese, Japanese and Korean, also taking into consideration the size of Asia and its growing economies
- We should capitalize on heritage speakers because they are a tremendous economic asset and train them to use their language skills in a professional environment
- Schools should not take away the students' native language but rather use them as a competitive advantage

### Cultural Competency

- Knowledge of cultural differences is imperative for effective communication especially when it comes to business
- Professional dealings with clients and colleagues in other countries require more than just an understanding of the language

## Lack of Awareness

- College graduates are unable to comprehend the importance of learning another language in an increasingly global society
- Businesses do not reward employees for proficiency in other languages, however, large companies like P&G, Intel and IBM are beginning to compensate employees who learn foreign languages

## Costs of Insufficient Language Capacity

- The opportunity cost of not understanding another language and culture is that it limits a company's external customer base and growth
- The dependency on translators is expensive and companies do not have the time to react quickly to situations should it arise, especially in a global market
- Businesses cannot even recognize a good opportunity should it even arise
- From the government's point of view, clients who cannot speak English cannot access the services even though they are available and legally entitled to
- Medical conditions cannot be diagnosed properly if patients do not speak English
- Court cases have to be delayed if translators are not available and in some cases, civil rights may have violated thus adding to the increase of lawsuits
- Many agencies have resorted to hiring private translators or reassigning employees to areas where there is a greater need thus increasing the inefficiency of the organization

## LANGUAGE ROADMAP FOR THE 21ST CENTURY

### Goal 1: Raise Public Awareness

(Parents & Communities, Public Education, Business, Government)

*Awareness*

- Establish a Texas Language Roadmap Coordinating Board, the first task of which is to conduct a large-scale survey and suggest a funding strategy
- Outline a public information campaign on the economic and cognitive benefits of language learning tailored to different audiences
- Analyze employer survey data, gather additional information, and develop documentation illustrating economic benefits of a multilingual workforce
- Launch a campaign geared to parents and the public at large on the cognitive benefits of language learning
- Launch an economic benefits campaign and disseminate information trough business organizations, trade associations, and PSAS

## Goal 2: Increase Instructional Capacity

(Public and Higher Education and Government)

### *Certification*

- Determine the need for teaching certificates in additional languages
- Add new certificates and certification exams as needed
- Periodically review the passing rate of exams

### *Proficiency*

- Identify existing proficiency certification prep courses for probationary and pre-service teachers
- Increase the numbers of prep courses and languages available, as needed
- Periodically evaluate courses' success-rates and revise the curriculum, as needed

### *Teacher Ed Curriculum*

- Key universities review the current teacher curriculum in light of state standards
- Revise the curriculum as needed to align with state standards and reflect language acquisition research
- Make revised curriculum models available to other institutions

### *Curriculum for Language Majors*

- Education and foreign language departments at major teacher-training institutions begin discussions on the restructuring of the language major
- Collaborative effort to create integrative, cross-disciplinary language major including study abroad
- Implement new language major program and share structure with other institutions
- Review the effectiveness of the language major curriculum and revise, as necessary

## Goal 3: Develop Advanced Linguistic and Cultural Proficiency

(Parents & Communities, Public and Higher Education, Business and Government)

### *Early Start Initiative*

- School district and community partnerships investigate and select an early language learning model
- School districts begin implementing chosen model
- Periodically evaluate students' proficiency and revise models, as needed

### *Extended Sequence*

- Expand existing programs for heritage speakers
- Add heritage speaker programs in additional school districts
- Increase the number of special-purposes course offerings, such as Chinese for Business

### *Structural Change*

- Add Languages Other than English (LOTE) to the foundation curriculum
- Establish a P-16 language articulated curriculum
- Implement the P-16 articulated curriculum

### *Enrichment Options*

- Expand service opportunities in which students use language skills in the community
- Add language service opportunities in additional school districts
- Establish International Language Academies in select districts

## Goal 4: Create Incentive Structures

(Public and Higher Education, Business and Government)

### *Study Incentives*

- Develop written policies awarding benefits to employees with advanced language skills
- Establish business and higher education partnerships to organize work/study options for students with advanced language skills
- Begin offering discipline-specific internships to students with advanced language Proficiency

### *Tax Credits*

- Provide tax incentives to businesses for investment in programs to enhance employees' language proficiency

### *Government Initiatives*

- Add Languages Other than English (LOTE) to Texas Governor's School Program
- Establish a state Language Service Corps Office to identify agencies most in need of employees with language skills and develop program and incentives accordingly

- Begin offering Language Service Corps positions to college graduates with advanced language skills
- Include language proficiency as a licensing requirement in critical fields like health care

## CURRENT LANGUAGE CAPACITIES AND LIMITATIONS

### Foreign Language Education in Texas

- According to the Texas Education Agency (2007), roughly 40% of the state's 7th to 12th graders were enrolled in a language class during the past school year
- A new state mandate requires all high school students to take at least 2 credits (a minimum of 2 years of study) in a foreign language in order to graduate (graduating class of 2008 will be the first to be affected)
- Spanish leads the way in the 15-plus languages taught and accounts for 81% of the total student enrollment in second language classes
- Top 5 languages taught are Spanish, French, German, Latin and American Sign Language
- Others languages taught are Spanish for Native Speakers, Japanese, Chinese, Russian, Italian, Hebrew, Arabic and Hindi
- According to the Texas Two-Way/Dual Language Consortium (2007), there are 255 twoway/dual language programs in Texas districts (see directory in appendix)
- The Center for Applied Linguistics (2006) reports that there are 8 Spanish and 1 French immersion programs in Texas (see directory attached in appendix)
- TEA indicates that less than 3% of elementary students in Texas study a foreign language even though this is the best opportunity for them to develop future language proficiency, excluding students in dual-language and bilingual programs

### Extent of Language Learning

- For those who begin a language, less than a quarter go on to the 3$^{rd}$ level and about 2% actually go on to the 4th level so the proficiency level is actually falling short
- Only 1.3% of all 2004 university graduates majored in a foreign language
- Less than 1% at UT Austin graduates with a foreign language in 2007

### Between Needs and Capacity

- All indications show that Texas is not currently equipped to meet the needs for foreign language speakers, let alone future demands
- Less than half of Texas public school students in grades 7–12 are enrolled in second language classes, the majority of whom will end their studies after two years

## Language Acquisition and Age

- The ability to develop advanced proficiency in a language is directly related to the length of time spent studying the language
- Children who are exposed to other languages and cultures at an early age tend to be more open to cultural differences
- After the age of 10, they begin to have stereotyped views of people they see as "other"
- Very few Texas students have the formal opportunity to begin learning another language therefore their language skills fall short of professional proficiency requirements

## Integration of Language and Cultural Learning

- To better understand another culture, it is best to raise the interest at an early age rather than wait till high school, as it is the case with Texas students

## Making Language Learning Practical

- Tie foreign language skills to functional skills and field-specific content, such as specialized terms used in law, medicine, engineering, criminal justice and other professional fields
- Texas secondary and high schools need to take this into account or else government and business agencies will bear the cost later when attempting to train employees in these areas

## Re-Valuing Languages Other Than English

- Heritage speakers have the natural advantage, however, few school districts see informal knowledge of heritage languages as a building block for formal language acquisition

# HOW DOES TEXAS RANK IN THE NUMBER OF CRITICAL LANGUAGE SPEAKERS?

- Urdu – ranked 2nd, after NY
- Chinese – ranked 3rd, after CA and NY
- Persian – ranked 3rd, after CA and VA
- Gujarathi – ranked 4th, after NJ, CA and IL
- Hindi – ranked 4th, after CA, NY and NJ
- Japanese – ranked 5th, after CA, HI, NY and WA

- Arabic – ranked 6th, after CA, MI, NY, NJ and IL
- Korean – ranked 6th, after CA, NY, NJ, IL and VA
- Russian – ranked 14th, after NY, CA, NJ, WA, PA, MA, IL, FL, MD, OR, GA, CO and OH
- The majority of the critical language speakers identify themselves as fluent English speakers and between the ages of 18–64. The number of fluent English speakers dramatically increases among the ages 5–17.
- Source: 2005 American Community Survey, http://www.mla.org/map_data

## NUMBER AND PERCENTAGE OF SPEAKERS PER LANGUAGE IN TEXAS

| | | |
|---|---|---|
| 13,230,765 | 68% | English |
| 6,010,753 | 32% | All languages other than English combined |
| 5,195,182 | 26% | Spanish or Spanish Creole |
| 122,517 | 0.64% | Vietnamese |
| 91,500 | 0.48% | Chinese |
| 82,117 | 0.43% | German |
| 62,274 | 0.32% | French (incl. Patois, Cajun) |
| 39,988 | 0.21% | Tagalog |
| 38,451 | 0.20% | Korean |
| 36,087 | 0.19% | African languages |
| 32,978 | 0.17% | Urdu |
| 32,909 | 0.17% | Arabic |
| 20,919 | 0.11% | Hindi |
| 19,140 | 0.10% | Gujarathi |
| 17,558 | 0.09% | Persian |
| 14,701 | 0.08% | Japanese |
| 11,574 | 0.06% | Russian |
| 11,158 | 0.06% | Italian |
| 10,378 | 0.05% | Laotian |
| 9,716 | 0.05% | Portuguese or Portuguese Creole |
| 9,652 | 0.05% | Polish |
| 7,870 | 0.04% | Mon-Khmer, Cambodian |
| 7,282 | 0.04% | Thai |
| 6,731 | 0.03% | Serbo-Croatian |
| 6,583 | 0.03% | Scandinavian languages |
| 6,571 | 0.03% | Greek |
| 4,622 | 0.02% | Hebrew |
| 3,603 | 0.02% | Other Native North American languages |
| 3,504 | 0.02% | French Creole |
| 2,140 | 0.01% | Hungarian |
| 1,172 | 0.01% | Armenian |

| 905 | <.01% | Yiddish |
| 595 | <.01% | Navajo |
| 180 | <.01% | Miao, Hmong |

Source: The Modern Language Association Language Map, 2000 United States Census Map, *http://www.mla.org/map_single*

# DUAL LANGUAGE EDUCATION

There are four main types of dual language (literacy and content) programs, which mainly differ in the population:

**Developmental,** or maintenance, bilingual programs. These enroll primarily students who are native speakers of the partner language.

**Two-way (bilingual) immersion** programs. These enroll a balance of native English speakers and native speakers of the partner language. (See directory in appendix)

**Foreign language immersion**, language immersion or one-way immersion. These enroll primarily native English speakers. This is a method of teaching a second language. (See directory in appendix)

**Heritage language programs.** These mainly enroll students who are dominant in English but whose parents, grandparents, or other ancestors spoke the partner language.

*Dual language programs are different from transitional bilingual programs, where the aim is to transition students out of their native language.*

# BEST PRACTICES

The UTeach Program at The University of Texas at Austin advocates using the targeted language to teach content/subject(eg. History or Literature) as being more effective than traditional language instruction on grammar.

## Northside Independent School District, San Antonio

- Students and families make a minimum 6-year commitment to the Dual Language Immersion Program
- Optimum classroom is 50% English speakers and 50% Spanish speakers
- Students receive instruction 90% in Spanish and 10% in English in Kindergarten and 1$^{st}$ grade, the Spanish instruction then decreases by 10% for each increasing grade
- Instructional delivery is monolingual at all times and teachers do not use translation for comprehension
- Teachers have high levels of proficiency in the target language
- Parents volunteer in activities to promote the program and work with their children at home

- Parents encourage the child's second language learning efforts and provide reading materials in 2 languages at home as well as attend dual language functions
- The results were impressive. English-speaking students were placed at Level III AP in middle school, 90% of Spanish-speaking students achieved Advanced or Advanced High on the Reading Proficiency Test in English; 100% of 6th graders passed TAKS and 95% passed the math portion of TAKS

## Alicia Chacon International School, El Paso

- Two-way immersion magnet program
- Children study English, Spanish and a 3rd language (Chinese, Japanese, German or Russian)
- Begins in Kindergarten with 80% Spanish, 10% English, 10% 3rd language
- Changes at grades 3, 5 and 7 to end with a 30/60/10 model
- Math and reading scores for students at Chacon were higher than scores for both the district and state as a whole

## TEXAS DUAL LANGUAGE PROGRAM COST ANALYSIS

### Report Developed for the Texas Education Agency and the Texas Senate Education Committee

*Mean Per-Pupil Costs for Start-Up, Annual and Additional Funds Needed by Program Size*

| Program Size | Start-Up | Annual | Additional |
|---|---|---|---|
| Small Program (n=27) | $825.00 | $879.00 | $568.00 |
| Med. Program (n=31) | $399.00 | $406.00 | $209.00 |
| Large Program (n=25) | $312.00 | $290.00 | $197.00 |

> *Note: Small Programs* = *0-120 Students;*
> *Medium Programs* = *121-240 Students;*
> *Large Programs* = *240+*
> *Students; Start-Up* = *Costs required to initiate program;*
> *Annual* = *yearly program costs;*
> *Additional* = *additional funds requested to maintain adequate program.*

The above data reveals that

- Smaller programs (0-120 students) were more costly per pupil to operate in all three categories: start-up, annual, and additional funds requested
- Large programs were the most cost effective in all three categories

- Large programs spent approximately 1/3 of the amount per pupil compared to small programs
- Reasons for cost effectiveness of larger programs:
  due to minimized teacher and student recruitment for the program
  shared resources, materials and administrative costs
  reduced staff development and certification costs
  larger percent of bilingual students in the district with associated Title III allotments
  a history of bilingual education programs and funding therefore having opportunities to have previously purchased bilingual materials

Source: http://ldn.tamu.edu/Archives/CBAReport.pdf

# TEXAS LANGUAGE ROADMAP ADVISORY BOARD

## Pascal D. Forgione, Jr., Ph.D.

### Superintendent of the Austin Independent School District

Pascal D. Forgione, Jr., Ph.D., has served as Superintendent of the Austin Independent School District since August 1999. Working with the District's Board of Trustees, Dr. Forgione has overseen continuously improving student academic achievement, the return to fiscal stability and a high bond rating for the district, two successful bond elections, and improved community support for Austin public schools. Dr. Forgione has announced his intention to retire as AISD Superintendent in June 2009.

Advisory Board Chair

Dr. Forgione has served as a chief education officer at the local, state and national levels. From 1996-99, he was U.S. Commissioner of Education Statistics with the National Center for Education Statistics (NCES) in the U.S. Department of Education. From 1991-96, he served as State Superintendent for Public Instruction for the State of Delaware.

Dr. Forgione began his career in education as a high school social studies teacher in the Baltimore City Public Schools. He earned a Doctorate in Administration and Policy Analysis from Stanford University in 1977, a Master's Degree in Urban History from Stanford in 1973, a Master's Degree in Educational Administration from Loyola College in 1969, a Bachelor's Degree in Theology from St. Mary's Seminary and University in 1968, and a Bachelor's Degree in Philosophy from St. Mary's Seminary and University in 1966.

Dr. Forgione serves on the Board of Directors of Austin Partners in Education, the Boys and Girls Clubs of Austin, and the Austin Symphony. He is a member of the Education and Workforce Committee of the Greater Austin Chamber of Commerce, the Education Committee of the Austin Area Research Organization (AARO), and the Board of Visitors of Southwestern University. He is also a member of the Greater Austin Hispanic Chamber of Commerce and the Capital City and African American Chamber of Commerce. He is on the Executive Committee of the Council of Great City Schools.

Dr. Forgione has served on the Board of Directors of the Austin Area Urban League, the National Board for Professional Teaching Standards and the Scholastic National Advisory Council. He also served as a consultant to, or member of, numerous educational organizations and initiatives including the Council of Chief State School Officers; National Center for Education and the Economy; National Council for Measurement in Education; the College Board; RAND Corporation; U.S. Department of Defense; Council for Basic Education; American Educational Research Association; and the National Governors Association. Dr. Forgione lives in Austin with his wife, Dr. Kaye Forgione, a national education consultant. He has three grown sons.

## Aaron Demerson

### Executive Director, Office of the Governor of Texas–Economic Development and Tourism

Aaron S. Demerson currently serves as the Executive Director of the Governor's Economic Development and Tourism Division. He has also served as the Director of Texas Business Development and as the Director of Administration when it was the Texas Economic Development agency.

Advisory Board Member

Prior to his re-employment with Economic Development & Tourism he served as the Manager of the state's innovative prepaid tuition program (The Texas Tomorrow Fund) at the

State Comptrollers Office. He has served in a number of areas within Economic Development & Tourism including the Small Business Division as a Small Business Consultant, and Manager of Credit Administration (Finance Division). He has also been employed as a Commercial Finance Analyst and Loan Administration Officer with Texas Bank in San Antonio.

Demerson has a BBA in Finance from Texas A&M University-Kingsville (formally A&I), received a general banking diploma from the American Institute of Banking.

# Rob Eissler

### Texas House of Representatives

Rob Eissler is the President of Eissler and Associates, an executive recruiting firm based in his hometown of twenty-five years, The Woodlands, Texas. He received a B.A. in Architecture from Princeton University, and then served his country as a carrier-based attack pilot on the USS John F. Kennedy in the United States Navy.

Advisory Board Member

Representative Eissler has spent twenty two years dedicated to the public education system of Texas, 18 of which were on the Conroe Independent School District Board of Trustees, including two terms as President.

In 1999, he was named one of 25 Original Hometown Heroes for The Woodlands by The Woodlands Villager/Courier newspapers and The Woodlands Operating Company, L.P. The Chamber of Commerce named him Citizen of the Year in 1999, where he served as the Chairman of the Board in 1988. Mr. Eissler has also served as the President of the Woodlands Rotary Club and as a board member of the South Montgomery Y.M.C.A. He coached youth sports for twenty years and is well known as one of the voices of High School Football on the local radio broadcast of area games.

Mr. Eissler was elected to represent District 15 as State Representative in November of 2002. In his third session, he was appointed to serve as Chairman of the Public Education Committee. Representative Eissler has been named Legislator of the Year by the Texas Council of Special Education Administrators, received The Texas Foreign Language

Association's Distinguished Public Service Award, The Texas Art Education Association's Governmental Award for Meritorious Service in the Arts, The Texas Music Educators Association Distinguished Service Award and the Champion for Free Enterprise Award by the Texas Association of Business three times and the Vocational Agriculture Teachers Outstanding Legislature Award. In May, 2005 Representative Eissler was named one of the Top Texas Legislators of the 79th Legislative Session by Capitol Inside. He was presented with the Star Award by Texans Standing Tall in recognition of his efforts during the 79th Legislature to reduce and prevent the consequences of underage alcohol use and binge drinking. He has served on committees for the Southern Regional Education Board comprised of 16 states and was recently appointed by the Governor to their Board. He has received the STAR award from the Texas Classroom Teachers Association twice.

He was recently listed as Honorable Mention in Texas Monthly magazine's Ten Best Legislators issue. Governor Perry appointed Representative Eissler to the Education Commission of the States in October of 2007 where he will represent Texas as one of 7 Commissioners. In February, 2008, he was awarded Legislative Advocate of the Year by the Texas PTA and the 2008 Friend of Texas Children Award from United Ways of Texas.

Rob and his wife Linda have three adult children and are members of The Woodlands United Methodist Church.

## Admiral Bobby Ray Inman

**The University of Texas at Austin Lyndon B. Johnson Centennial Chair in National Policy**

Admiral Bobby R. Inman, USN (Ret.), graduated from the University of Texas at Austin in 1950, and from the National War College in 1972. He became an adjunct professor at the University of Texas at Austin in 1987. He was appointed as a tenured professor holding the Lyndon B. Johnson Centennial Chair in National Policy in August 2001. From January 1 through December 31, 2005, he served as Interim Dean of the LBJ School.

Advisory Board Member

Admiral Inman served in the U.S. Navy from November 1951 to July 1982, when he retired with the permanent rank of Admiral. While on active duty he served as Director of the National Security Agency and Deputy Director of Central Intelligence. After retirement from the Navy, he was Chairman and Chief Executive Officer of the Microelectronics and Computer Technology Corporation (MCC) in Austin, Texas for four years and Chairman, President and Chief Executive Officer of Westmark Systems, Inc., a privately owned electronics industry holding company for three years. Admiral Inman also served as Chairman of the Federal Reserve Bank of Dallas from 1987 through 1990.

Admiral Inman's primary activity since 1990 has been investing in start-up technology companies, where he is Chairman and a Managing Partner of Gefinor Ventures. He is a member of the Board of Directors of Massey Energy Company and several privately held companies. He serves as a Trustee of the American Assembly and the California Institute of Technology. He is a Director of the Public Agenda Foundation and is an elected fellow of the National Academy of Public Administration.

## Mark Strama

### Texas House of Representatives

Elected to the Texas House of Representatives in 2004, Mark Strama is a native Texan who has divided his career between public service and private business, always fighting to empower voters and make government more responsive to every American.

Advisory Board Member

After graduating from Brown University, he worked on Ann Richards' successful 1990 campaign for governor. He went on to become chief of staff for State Senator Rodney Ellis. During Mark's tenure, Senator Ellis was named one of the ten best legislators in the state by *Texas Monthly*. In 1995, Mark left government to become director of programs at Rock the Vote, where he helped register more than a million new voters.

Mark returned to Austin to found the first company to register voters online. Working to bring the economy, efficiency, and convenience of new technology to the democratic process, Mark's company was acquired by New York-based Election.com in 2000, and helped over 700,000 Americans register to vote in the 2000 election cycle.

Mark has served on the Board of Directors of KidsVoting USA, a national non-profit organization that develops civics education programs for K-12 students. He was a founding board member of Hope Street Group, a non-partisan organization of young business leaders that seeks to achieve equality of opportunity in a high-growth economy.

Mark is a member of the Greater Pflugerville Chamber of Commerce and the Pflugerville Council of Neighborhood Associations. He is also a founding member of the Pflugerville ISD MEN in Education program, which places male volunteers in schools to serve as mentors and role models.

With a broad range of experience in the business sector, non-profit sector, and in government, Mark is a voice for independence and integrity in the Texas Legislature. He advocates comprehensive reforms to the political system, so that politicians will place the public interest above special interests to improve our schools, health care, transportation systems, and economy.

Mark and his wife, Crystal, are the proud parents of Victoria Rose Strama who was born in January of 2007.

## APPENDIX

**Directory of Two-Way Bilingual Immersion Programs in Texas as of August 25, 2008 (K-12)**

The programs listed in this Directory meet all three of the following criteria for two-way immersion (TWI) programs:

**Integration:** Language-minority and language-majority students are integrated for at least 50% of instructional time at all grade levels

**Instruction:** Content and literacy instruction in English and the partner language is provided to all students, and *all students receive instruction in the partner language at least 50% of the instructional day*

**Population:** Within the program, there is a balance of language-minority and languagemajority students, with each group making up between one-third and two-thirds of the total student population

**Canutillo Middle Program Enhancement Canutillo, TX**
**Language used:** Spanish
**Basic model:** Middle or High

**Bellaire High School Project BLISS**
Bellaire, TX
**Language used:** Spanish
**Basic model:** Middle or High

**Bill Childress Program Enhancement Project**
Canutillo, TX
**Language used:** Spanish
**Basic model:** Balanced

**Canutillo Program Enhancement Project**
Canutillo, TX
**Language used:** Spanish
**Basic model:** Balanced

**Deanna Davenport Program Enhancement Project**
Canutillo, TX
**Language used:** Spanish
**Basic model:** Balanced

**Jose Alderete Middle School: Program Enhancement**
Canutillo, TX
**Language used:** Spanish
**Basic model:** Middle or High

**Jose Damian Program Enhancement Project**
Canutillo, TX

## Directory of Foreign Language Immersion Programs

This directory includes elementary, middle, and high schools that teach all or part of their curriculum through a second language. Such programs are referred to as total or partial immersion programs. In general, the programs are designed for students whose native language is English.

*Total Immersion*
Programs in which all subjects taught in the lower grades (K-2) are taught in the foreign language; instruction in English usually increases in the upper grades (3-6) to 20%-50%, depending on the program.

*Partial Immersion*
Programs in which up to 50% of subjects are taught in the foreign language; in some programs, the material taught in the foreign language is reinforced in English.

*Two-Way Immersion*
Programs that give equal emphasis to English and non-English language and in which one to two thirds of the students are native speakers of the non-English language, with the remainder being native speakers of English.

**Alamo Heights Junior School**
San Antonio, TX
**Language used:** Spanish
**Basic model:** Partial

**Cambridge Elementary School**
San Antonio, TX
**Language used:** Spanish
**Basic model:** Total

**Dawson Elementary School**
Corpus Christi, TX
**Language used:** Spanish
**Basic model:** Partial

**Dr. Alejo Salinas, Jr. Elementary School**
Hidalgo, TX
**Language used:** Spanish
**Basic model:** Total

**Forth Worth Independent School**
Fort Worth, TX
**Language used:** Spanish
**Basic model:** Partial

**Petite Ecole International**
Austin, TX

In: Building Strategic Language Ability Programs
Editor: Joshua R. Weston
ISBN: 978-1-60741-127-7
© 2010 Nova Science Publishers, Inc.

**Chapter 4**

# STATEMENT OF ROBERT O. SLATER, NATIONAL SECURITY EDUCATION PROGRAM BEFORE THE HOUSE ARMED SERVICES COMMITTEE, SUBCOMMITTEE ON OVERSIGHT AND INVESTIGATIONS

## INTRODUCTION AND BACKGROUND

Mr. Chairman and members of this distinguished committee, thank you for the opportunity to speak with you on the National Security Education Program's (NSEP's) role in support of the Department of Defense language transformation effort and the broader goals of the National Security Language Initiative.

You have requested that I focus on issues related to NSEP's role in the DoD language transformation plan and the National Security Language Initiative.

It is important to note as historical background that NSEP was the product of lessons learned from a series of 1991 post-Desert Storm Congressional hearings. The stark realization from these hearings was that our nation continually suffers from a lack of capacity to understand and communicate effectively in other languages and with other cultures. We were reminded during other crises of this lack of capacity and, of course, the events of 9/11 and the crises in Iraq and Afghanistan, as well as those throughout the rest of the globe, have underscored the compelling need for an entirely new generation of global professionals – who have the capacity to more effectively communicate in a wide array of critical languages and who are adept and adroit in regional and local culture. While NSEP's role in addressing critical shortfalls in these areas was recognized and well chronicled during the 1990s, the emergence of the Defense Language Transformation Roadmap, the Quadrennial Defense Review, and the National Security Language Initiative helped focus more attention on the critical role that the program has played – and can play – in addressing the larger contextual needs for this expertise.

NSEP represents an important commitment from within the Department of Defense (and the national intelligence community) to partner with U.S. education to dramatically improve the global expertise of those entering the federal workforce. NSEP has become a focal point for the Department's investment in creating a pipeline of linguistically and culturally competent professionals into the national security workforce. We recognize that in order to increase language capability in the Department – and achieve higher levels of language proficiency among our language professions, we must assume a more proactive role in promoting and encouraging foreign language education in the American population.

While a relatively small piece of the overall puzzle, NSEP's contribution to the overall national capacity – and to national security – is vital.

Today, NSEP consists of five critical component programs:

1. *NSEP Boren Undergraduate Scholars.* Since 1994, a program of scholarships to outstanding U.S. undergraduate students to study critical languages and cultures.
2. *NSEP Boren Graduate Fellowships.* Since 1994, a program of fellowships to outstanding U.S. graduate students to study critical languages and cultures.
3. *Language Flagship.* Since 2001, a strategic partnership with U.S. education to develop and implement high quality programs graduating students at professional levels of proficiency in languages critical to national security.
4. *English for Heritage Language Speakers.* Since 2006, a program offering U.S. citizens who are native speakers of critical languages an opportunity to develop higher levels of English proficiency.
5. *National Language Service Corps (NLSC).* Since 2007, the development of a pilot for an entirely new organization composed of U.S. citizens with critical language skills available to the federal government during times of emergency or national need.

In addition to these programs, NSEP works in close collaboration with the Defense Language Office to achieve other goals critical to the language transformation plan including an effort to build language and culture learning opportunities for ROTC cadets.

NSEP includes a rather unique and important statutory requirement as a component of its scholarship and fellowship awards – a requirement that the award recipient seek work in a national security related position in the federal government (and in first priority in DoD, State, Homeland Security, or ODNI) as a condition of accepting the award. We are delighted to report that there is no shortage of highly talented and outstanding American university students who are motivated to apply to NSEP for support not only because they seek funding to study critical languages but are eager to contribute to national security.

At least 1,200 NSEP Scholars and Fellows are now or have completed their federal service requirements. Their contributions to the departments of the federal government engaged in issues relating to national security have been enormous. As an example, on Sept 22 NSEP recognized the accomplishments of two outstanding former Undergraduate Scholars and Graduate Fellows in a major ceremony and reception:

*Matthew Parin*, a 2005 Boren Scholar, studied Arabic in Egypt. Matthew currently works in the Middle East & North Africa Office at the Department of Defense. He previously interned with the Federal Aviation Administration, where he worked on the Middle East desk in the Office of International Aviation.

*Benjamin Orbach,* a 2002 Boren Fellow, studied Arabic in Jordan. His experiences as a Boren Fellow formed the basis for a book, *Live from Jordan: Letters Home from My Journey*

*Through the Middle East.* He now works for the Department of State and serves in the Office of the Middle East Partnership Initiative, including on assignment to the U.S. Consulate in Jerusalem, and has received multiple professional awards.

NSEP award recipients are already establishing major and highly visible careers throughout the national security community.

*NSEP's Role in the DoD Language Transformation Plan and the National Security Language Initiative*

NSEP's mission has expanded dramatically throughout the current decade. In 2004, the Department of Defense in close collaboration with the Center for Advanced Study of Language at the University of Maryland, sponsored a major National Language Conference bringing together, for the first time, senior representatives from national, state, and local education organizations, federal agencies, and business to address this vital issue. The conference led to the publication of a White Paper, published by the Department, outlining a number of key recommendations.

In many ways, the 2004 Conference and resulting White Paper functioned as important catalysts for the formation of a working group, initially composed of representatives from the Departments of Defense, Education, and State. This high level group was committed – with the strong support of the three Department Secretaries – to develop a plan that would dramatically increase the number of Americans learning critical need foreign languages. The plan was formally announced by the President in January 2006 as the National Security Language Initiative (NSLI).

NSEP executes the DoD component of NSLI. Equally important, NSEP's expanded efforts are major components of DoD's language transformation plan. In addition to ongoing NSEP efforts to fund and place highly qualified award recipients in national security related positions, NSEP focuses on two major components in its role in both NSLI and the DoD language transformation plan: (1) Dramatically expanding the reach of the Language Flagship Program; (including State Language Roadmaps) and (2) building the pilot National Language Service Corps.

### The Language Flagship

During the era we generally categorize as "post 9/11," consensus has emerged that the American education system must more aggressively embrace the concept of global education for a broader population of students. The products of American education generally remain woefully unprepared to engage in a rapidly changing socio-economic and political environment that demands global skills. The most needed of these is the ability to effectively engage in languages other than English.

Since its inception in 2000, The Department of Defense Language Flagship initiative has provided important funding to the American higher education system to re-tool its approaches to language education. At the core of the Flagship concept is the assumption that the development of global skills (including advanced language competency) must be mainstreamed into American education. Ultimately, any approach to achieving language competency must begin as early as pre-school and, like other curricula, be defined as an articulated process from elementary, middle, and high school into the university. The long-term vision of The Language Flagship is a system where high school graduates emerge with intermediate to advanced competencies in languages ranging from Arabic to Chinese to

Swahili and find opportunities and incentives to continue their language training toward professional proficiency as undergraduates. Flagship Centers enroll students drawn from all majors including business, engineering, and science. The Language Flagship envisions an array of colleges and universities across the U.S. known for their advanced language programs in concert with other vital efforts to establish a pipeline of students from K-12 into the university.

## What Is the Language Flagship?

The Language Flagship represents the beginnings of a proactive community of innovators comprised of a system of 13 domestic Flagship Centers and three K-12 programs, as well as 7 overseas Flagship Centers in places such as Alexandria Egypt, Nanjing, China, and St. Petersburg, Russia. The Language Flagship also consists of a rapidly expanding group of partners in higher education and business across the United States. This community is led by nationally-recognized leaders and innovators in language education.

The Language Flagship is a federally-funded effort and is a component of the National Security Education Program (NSEP) at the U.S Department of Defense. It began in late 2000 as a small pilot project to challenge a few U.S. colleges and universities to investigate their capacity and commitment to build programs of advanced language acquisition.[1] Important opportunities were developed for a small cohort of students to engage in one- to two-year post-BA language programs that included an intensive year of language study in the U.S. followed by an articulated program of overseas study that included internships and direct enrollment in content courses taught in the target language.

Between 2001, when the first pilot grants were awarded, and 2005, the effort expanded to include additional universities offering programs in Arabic, Chinese, Korean, Persian, and Russian. In addition to the post-BA pilot efforts, two undergraduate Flagship Centers were established to test the capacity of institutions to produce undergraduate students with professional-level language proficiency. The Flagship model was further tested by the establishment of a pilot K-12 Chinese Flagship program. This pilot K-12 initiative was expanded in January 2006 to add two K-12 programs in Arabic and Chinese as part of the President's National Security Language Initiative (NSLI). Flagship Centers for Hindi/Urdu and Central Asian Turkic languages were also added as part of NSLI. This fall Flagship will begin funding a new African Languages Center.

The results of these initial pilot efforts were highly encouraging. Institutions created highly effective programs and students rose to meet the challenge. However, it was clear that a post-BA model alone would mean that these efforts would remain limited and out of reach to most American students. It was also clear that truly changing the paradigm of language learning in the U.S. and achieving the Flagship goal to reach at least 2000 students by the end of the decade required mainstreaming curricula into students' undergraduate years and, at a minimum, articulating those curricula down to high schools.

Recognizing the potential of the Flagship model and the imperative to broaden opportunities for U.S. students, The Language Flagship in 2006 refocused its effort to include advanced, proficiency-based language instruction as an integral component of undergraduate education. By doing so, the Flagship model could address the needs of hundreds, if not thousands, of students who are motivated to gain professional proficiency in language during their undergraduate studies. In spring 2006, all Flagship Centers were asked to develop curricula that responded to the needs of undergraduates. The goals were simple yet highly challenging: build curricula that offer entering college freshman the opportunity to elect a track that moves them to professional proficiency regardless of their major.

The goals of The Language Flagship are ambitious. We seek to enroll a minimum of 2,000 students, nationwide, in Flagship programs by the end of the decade.

The Language Flagship effort focuses on six key elements:

- New curricular approaches
- K-12 articulation
- Articulated Overseas Language Immersion
- Diffusion of innovation to new institutions
- Peer review and quality assurance
- Engagement of the business sector

## New Curricular Approaches

Our experience developing Flagship Centers has demonstrated that existing language programs need to be radically re-engineered to achieve the goal of producing graduates of all majors with professional proficiency. The Language Flagship encourages a broad range of transformative activities with respect to curricular design, institutional enhancements, and commitments to advanced language programming. Key to the transformation of the curriculum is the commitment to the following principles: 1) new pathways to language learning; 2) evidence-based language learning; and 3) institutionalization and long-term sustainable change.

### *New Pathways to Language Learning*

Creating new pathways to language learning requires developing high-level language learning opportunities for a broad group of college and university students. Flagship students are unique because they represent a wide range of academic majors. Because of this model, Flagship programs have had to rethink the approach to undergraduate education to ensure that students are able to undertake study in their major while meeting the challenges involved in acquiring advanced language skills. Flagship Centers take these challenges into consideration in designing their method and approach to language learning.

New pathways to language learning require two important changes to the curriculum. One change is creating a language learning curriculum that meets the needs of language learners who wish to achieve professional proficiency. The second is creating a content-based curriculum for students in a variety of disciplines. In order for Flagship Centers to prepare students to use their language skills professionally in their field, they must collaborate with other academic departments and create experiential learning opportunities. Flagship curricula maximize the exposure to and use of the target language, drawing on partnerships with the full and best resources of each language field. Flagship Centers cooperate with campus units in other disciplines in both curricular design and program implementation. In addition to classroom learning, all Flagship Centers incorporate coordinated internships and/or community service into the overseas portion of students' study.

### Evidence-based Language Learning

Evidence-based learning is a means to measure our performance as well as that of the student. Flagship programs incorporate multiple means to assess student proficiency and performance and to routinely gather and share evidence about how well our learning interventions are working. In doing so, Flagship builds continuous cycles of improvement into language learning practices. At the same time, Flagship emphasizes the accumulation of knowledge gained from testing alternative learning strategies, particularly at the more advanced level. Flagship programs also emphasize diagnostic assessment which assists in placing students in programs and allows learning strategies to be tailored to the strengths and weaknesses of individual learners.

### Institutional Commitment and Long-term Sustainability

Through The Language Flagship, the Department of Defense has signaled its commitment to building an enduring infrastructure of programs across the nation that is fully integrated into the mainstream of higher education. As these programs involve a new approach to undergraduate language education, this infrastructure cannot exist without the strong interest and support of the highest levels of university leadership. At the most fundamental level, institutional commitment means that these programs must be reflected in the overall long-term strategic direction of the institution. Flagship Centers have had to address a number of challenges posed by traditional language learning structures and approaches to language learning in American higher education. Many of these problems were addressed in the 2007 report of the Modern Language Association (MLA), Ad Hoc Committee on Foreign Languages. Unlike the mainstream language departments, Flagship Centers have already put into place a number of solutions to the problems addressed in the report by the MLA. Most importantly, at the core of Flagship Centers are senior-level professors and experts in language acquisition.

## K-12 Articulation

Few countries face the challenges we do as a result of students only beginning to learn languages when they enter college. The average American student, even one who has benefited from an immersion environment, enters the university with only basic skills in a second language. The likelihood that the average high school graduate has an intermediate to advanced proficiency in a second language is highest for the European languages where a broader network of opportunities is available in the K-12 system. Few students come to the university with measurable skills in non-European languages.

The goal of The Language Flagship is not only to graduate students at a professionally proficient level of language but also to "push the model" down to elementary, middle, and high schools so that students will enter college with an established and measurable skill in a second language. Without such input, higher education programs will continue to devote limited resources to remedial efforts to prepare incoming students through pre-collegiate summer immersions and first-year "catch up" programs. These efforts are currently needed to bring students to a higher proficiency level, after which Flagship programs can integrate them into a more challenging and advanced curriculum. The integration of language skills into K-12 education is vital to our capacity to educate a citizenry prepared to address the nation's well being in the 21$^{st}$ century.

Sensitive to the need to provide leadership and direction, and as an integral component of a national effort to address language education, the Department has supported three groundbreaking efforts designed to model a K-12 language curriculum development and implementation process. These efforts, located at the University of Oregon (Chinese); Michigan State University (Arabic); and Ohio State University (Chinese) provide national models of articulated curricula designed to graduate high school students at the advanced level of proficiency.

Ultimately, the goal is the development of K-12 language instruction programs that graduate high school students with an advanced level of competency and that allow Flagship programs to take them to the next level. Flagship is working closely with each of its Centers and programs to improve the flow of more highly proficient language graduates into the university.

## Articulated Overseas Immersion

Evidence is compelling that students require an intensive and rigorous program of overseas study to reach the professional proficiency level as well as to develop the cultural skills that are associated with this level. The Language Flagship provides unparalleled opportunities for students to engage in carefully articulated programs of study that include advanced language instruction, direct enrollment in classes taught in the target language, specialized tutors, and internships involving practical use of the language.

Flagship Center directors work together in *Overseas Academic Councils* to design and implement curricula that address the needs of students matriculated at different institutions. The long-term goal of Flagship is to create an overseas infrastructure that can respond to a growing supply of students from throughout U.S. higher education who have demonstrated a proficiency level that qualifies them for intensive Flagship overseas study.

The overseas undergraduate immersion model assumes that students require a full-year program of overseas study once they have achieved an advanced level of proficiency. This fullyear immersion may take place during the third, fourth, or fifth year of a student's undergraduate program. The model also assumes that, in addition to full-year study, some students will require shorter periods of immersion overseas to accelerate their language learning and to accommodate academic schedules.

## Diffusion of Innovation

Diffusion of innovation is an important and well-documented approach to ensuring that innovations are effectively communicated and adopted throughout a system. At the core of Flagship is the commitment to a process that diffuses successful models throughout higher education. As such, Flagship follows a process that funds innovators to develop and implement new models of language learning, assessment, and standards development, and then share them with "early adopters." These early adopters are committed to move these innovations into new institutional settings. The model is designed to increase the scope and scale of advanced language learning by making Flagship language programs available to an increasing number of students across the U.S.

In order to promote diffusion of innovation, The Language Flagship offers grants to encourage new partnerships to engage in program development. During 2007-2008, The Language Flagship has actively sought to partner existing Flagship Centers with other committed institutions of higher education to "nationalize" the model of advanced language learning. This will not only assist The Language Flagship in reaching its goal of 2,000 enrolled students by the end of the decade but will export the lessons learned from this program more broadly into the national education system.

## Peer Review and Quality Assurance

The goals of The Language Flagship are closely tied to clear measures of success and outcomes that are common across all Flagship Centers. Though the methods and approaches of each Flagship Center may differ, the end result is the same: to produce college graduates from many different disciplines who are highly proficient in all modalities of language usage (speaking, reading, writing, and listening). Such goals call for the development of standards and methods of quality assurance that have been rare in language education in the American higher education system. Peer review is central in determining the standards a Flagship Center must meet.

Peer review provides a means for Flagship Center Directors to evaluate the quality of their Flagship peers. It ensures that directors learn from each other through close communication, student and faculty interviews, and discussions with staff. Through this process, The Language Flagship establishes a means of quality assurance and standards that help provide clear guidance for new institutions who wish to become part of The Language Flagship family.

## Engagement of the Business Sector

The Language Flagship has, since its inception, promoted the value of partnership between government, education, and business. Through such a partnership we are able to set the foundations for long-term financial sustainability as well as affect the way a variety of sectors value language in the workplace. Beginning in 2007, the Department of Defense through its flagship initiative, took the lead to coordinate the *2007: U.S. Language Summits: Roadmaps to Language Excellence*. I will discuss this Roadmap initiative later in my testimony. Flagship views businesses as future employers of its graduates, suppliers of crucial internship opportunities, and potential financial supporters.

# A CLOSER LOOK AT FLAGSHIP CENTERS

## Flagship Centers and Programs

The Language Flagship supports undergraduate and post-BA programs and a limited number of pilot K-12 programs. Flagship Centers are based at institutions around the United States and offer an on-campus curriculum coupled with a strategy for intensive study at an Overseas Flagship Center. Overseas Flagship Centers are located at participating foreign institutions and are coordinated by a lead Flagship Center. The Language Flagship supports three K-12 Flagship Programs at public schools in Ohio, Oregon, and Michigan. These pilot programs are intended to serve as a national model for articulated K-12 language instruction in the U.S.

### *Same Goal, Different Pathways*

Though all Flagship Centers have the same goal–to create graduates of American colleges and universities who are professionally proficient in key languages–each Flagship Center follows its own pathway to reaching that goal. These different pathways are based on a number of factors, the most important being the language offered, the methodological approach of the language experts, and the types of students enrolled. Chinese, for example, is a high demand language. This is reflected by the fact that The Language Flagship supports five different domestic Chinese Flagship Centers and programs as well as two different Overseas Centers. These Overseas Centers are coordinated by the Chinese Flagship Academic Council, which ensures that the structure and curriculum overseas is well articulated with the different domestic curricula. In addition, at least two of the five Chinese Flagship Centers work closely with Flagship-funded K-12 programs. Two Chinese Flagship Centers offer post-BA/graduate degrees.

On the other end of the spectrum, The Language Flagship approaches the teaching of smaller enrollment languages by focusing on language groupings, such as Central Asian Turkic languages, Eurasian languages, and African languages. Because these language groups represent low national enrollments, The Language Flagship approaches these languages through a partnership, or consortial, approach. Recognizing that no institution of higher education has a large number of students who are ready to learn these languages at the higher levels, these programs engage multiple partner institutions to create a critical mass of students. These students eventually study overseas at selected locations that can accommodate direct enrollment at universities.

The Flagship approach is based on flexibility. Flagship Centers are designed to accommodate students who enter the program at different levels of proficiency. Some Flagship Centers focus on attracting students who already have intermediate-level language skills. However, as Flagship Centers become more experienced in training students at the higher levels, they admit entering freshmen with no prior knowledge in the target language with the understanding that the student may have to take an extra year to reach professional proficiency.

Regardless of the language in which a student is enrolled, the pathway to proficiency ensures that students receive intensive, directed language and cultural instruction alongside their academic majors. Such an approach means that Flagship Centers need to reevaluate many long-standing policies shaping academic requirements, student financial aid, and overseas study.

### *Expansion*

In support of the National Security Language Initiative, the Department's goal has been to increase the scale and scope of the program to impact as many students as possible. Beginning in 2007 the program expanded Flagship by creating new Flagship Partner Programs through the Promoting Diffusion of Innovation grant program. These partner institutions join with Flagship Centers to implement Flagship curricula, but are not yet fully-fledged Flagship Centers. The first Flagship Partner Program was formed at Arizona State University; five additional partner programs have now been added. The Language Flagship plan is to aggressively seek and add new partners each year beginning in 2008 through our Diffusion of Innovation grant program.

## FLAGSHIP CENTERS

### African

Howard University and University of Wisconsin, Madison (September 2008)

### Arabic

Michigan State University
Dearborn Public Schools K–12 Arabic Program
University of Texas, Austin
University of Maryland, College Park
University of Michigan, Ann Arbor Flagship Partner Program
University of Oklahoma Flagship Partner Program
*Alexandria University, Egypt\**
*Damascus University, Syria\**

### Central Asian Turkic Languages Consortium

American Councils for International Education

### Chinese

Arizona State University Flagship Partner Program
Brigham Young University
Indiana University Flagship Partner Program
Ohio State University

Ohio Public Schools K–12 Flagship Program
University of Mississippi
University of Oregon
Portland Public Schools K–12 Flagship Program
*Nanjing University, China\**
*Qingdao University, China\**

## Eurasian Languages Consortium

American Councils for International Education
Bryn Mawr College
Middlebury College
Portland State University Flagship Partner Program
University of California, Los Angeles
University of Maryland, College Park
*Saint Petersburg State University, Russia\**

## Hindi/Urdu

University of Texas, Austin

## Korean

University of Hawai'i, Manoa
*Korea University, South Korea\**

## Persian/Farsi

University of Maryland, College Park
*Tajik State National University, Tajikistan\**

## Flagship Students

Flagship students at the K-12, undergraduate, and post-BA levels represent the next generation of global professionals in the United States. Students come from all regions of the nation and pursue their own academic interests in addition to language study.

The success of the Language Flagship has meant that the Centers have already begun attracting top students to their campuses. Flagship programs cater to students' individual

---

\* Overseas Flagship Center

proficiency levels, tailoring language instruction to meet the needs of each learner. This model has proven to be a successful approach to stimulating student interest and keeping students engaged in learning both language and culture. Retention in Flagship programs is high; the majority of students progress from year to year with greater language proficiency.

Flagship enrollments have doubled every year since 2003, however the program remained relatively small as a result of its focus on post-BA students. In 2007 Flagship added new undergraduate programs and enrolled 136 undergraduate students. Together with the Flagship post-BA program enrollment of 100 students, the total student enrollment in Flagship undergraduate and post-BA programs for 2007 was 236. In 2008 we will expand to add more undergraduate programs in Chinese, Korean, and Persian/Farsi. As depicted in **Chart 1**, we anticipate 349 students to enroll in these and existing undergraduate and post-BA Flagship programs. Of these 253 will be undergraduate students and 96 will be Post-BA students.

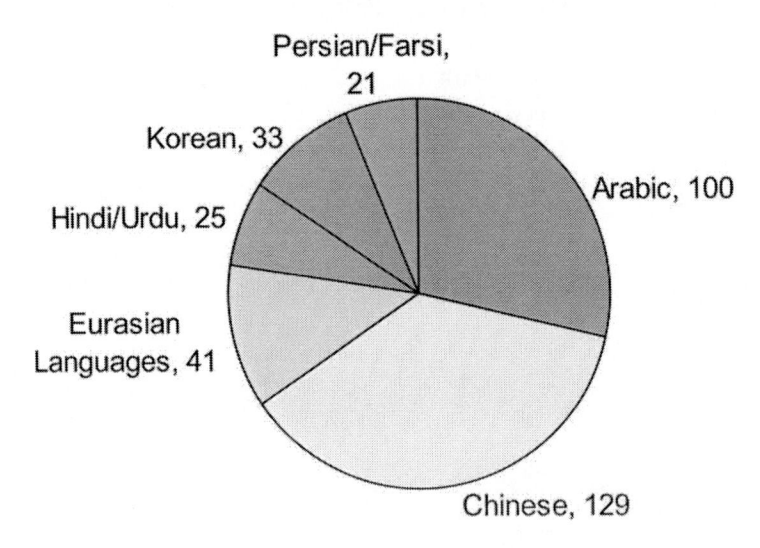

Chart 1. 2008 Projected Student Enrollment in Undergraduate and Post-BA Flagship Programs by Critical Language, n=349

## Flagship Student Profiles

Flagship students come from all parts of the United States with a variety of levels of language proficiency in a Flagship language. Students share the goal of reaching professional proficiency and using their language and culture skills to contribute to a global society. Each student is contributing to and fulfilling the Flagship vision in his or her own unique way. Below is a sampling of students who have joined the Flagship movement.

- A Flagship Scholar and junior at Michigan State University studies Arabic in the Flagship program and is majoring in Interdisciplinary Humanities. She plans to work in the field of international development using her Arabic skills.
- A post-BA Russian Flagship Fellow completed the overseas program at St. Petersburg State University and went on to interpret for U.S. and Russian personnel

for the Washington, D.C.-Moscow Presidential Hotline. He is now pursing a master's degree at Harvard University studying religious and ethnic issues, especially the interaction between Christianity and Islam in Central Asia.

- A Flagship Scholar and BS/MA senior in biochemistry and Chinese at Ohio State University was recently recognized as a member of the prestigious USA Today Academic First Team. He is currently studying traditional Chinese medicine in Beijing, China, and hopes to pursue a career in medicine with a focus on international public health.
- A post-BA Flagship Fellow in Korean and a student of mathematics at the University of Hawaii designed his own course of study in the Korean language with a Korean-speaking professor from University of Hawaii's College of Engineering. He went on to earn an MS in information security from Korea University and is currently working toward a Ph.D. in statistics from Ohio State University.
- A Flagship Scholar and senior from Brigham Young University is studying linguistics and Chinese studies at Nanjing University in China. She plans to pursue a law degree with a focus on international law.
- A post-BA Persian Flagship student is studying at the Dushanbe Language Center in Tajikistan. He is also proficient in French and hopes to work for the FBI in the Language Services Section.
- A post-BA Flagship Fellow completed the Arabic Flagship program at the University of Maryland. Previously she earned a master's degree from American University in Cairo, where she studied forced migration and refugee studies. She is now working for the Office for Civil Rights and Civil Liberties in the U.S. Department of Homeland Security.

## The Future of Flagship

Following the transition to undergraduate programs, The Language Flagship is growing rapidly and is beginning to change language learning at U.S. institutions of higher education. As we expand and diffuse Flagship innovations, more universities are recognizing that they want to change the way they teach languages. Students are embracing Flagship programs to prepare them for future careers as global professionals. Already, The Language Flagship has changed student expectations for undergraduate study. As The Language Flagship moves forward, increasing numbers of students will come to expect high-quality language programs as part of their undergraduate experience. Such expectations drive the market. Institutions hosting Flagship Centers have already seen the power of these programs as recruitment tools. This has been evident in the relatively short time that Flagship Centers have had to develop, implement, and recruit students. Though many of our Flagship undergraduate programs started as late as 2007, Flagship Centers have demonstrated on the whole a high level of interest and increased enrollment.

As mentioned above, one of the core goals of The Language Flagship is to increase its scale and scope by having existing Flagship Centers and programs work closely with interested adopters. **Chart 2** depicts the rapid growth of The Language Flagship projected to the year 2018, including enrollments in the undergraduate and post-BA programs. A conservative estimate is that Flagship programs will enroll no fewer than 600 students during the 2010-2011 academic year and meet the goal of reaching at least 2000 students by the end of the current decade.

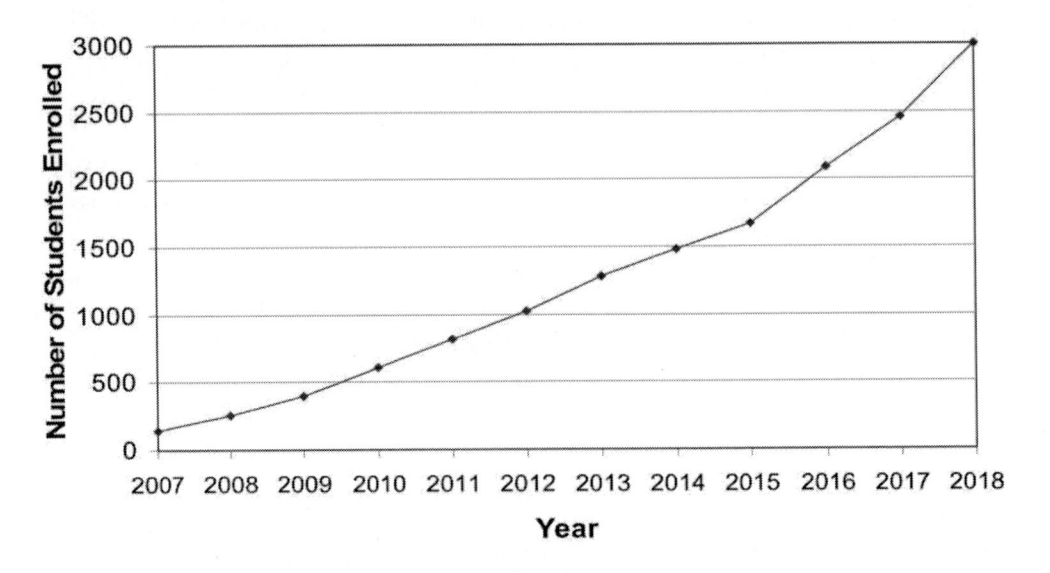

Chart 2. Undergraduate Enrollment Projections Through 2018

The Language Flagship is developing a growing national structure of U.S. colleges and universities offering advanced language opportunities to undergraduate students. **Chart 3** shows current and projected numbers of institutions involved in Flagship initiatives through 2018. These projections assume a conservative estimate of an additional four undergraduate programs funded through Diffusion of Innovation grants each year.

Flagship's involvement in K-12 language education is designed to provide a national model which school districts around the U.S. may embrace in the future. Although a small pilot initiative, K-12 Flagship programs have already demonstrated remarkable success in numbers of students impacted by The Language Flagship. We hope that the K-12 effort will expand to other school systems nationwide and that other forms of federal support will become available to assist in this transformation.

### State Language Roadmaps

DoD tasked NSEP in 2007 to sponsor a series of state strategic planning efforts that would effectively embrace the roadmap concept. We identified three candidate states where there were active Language Flagship programs that could effectively orchestrate the state strategic planning exercise.

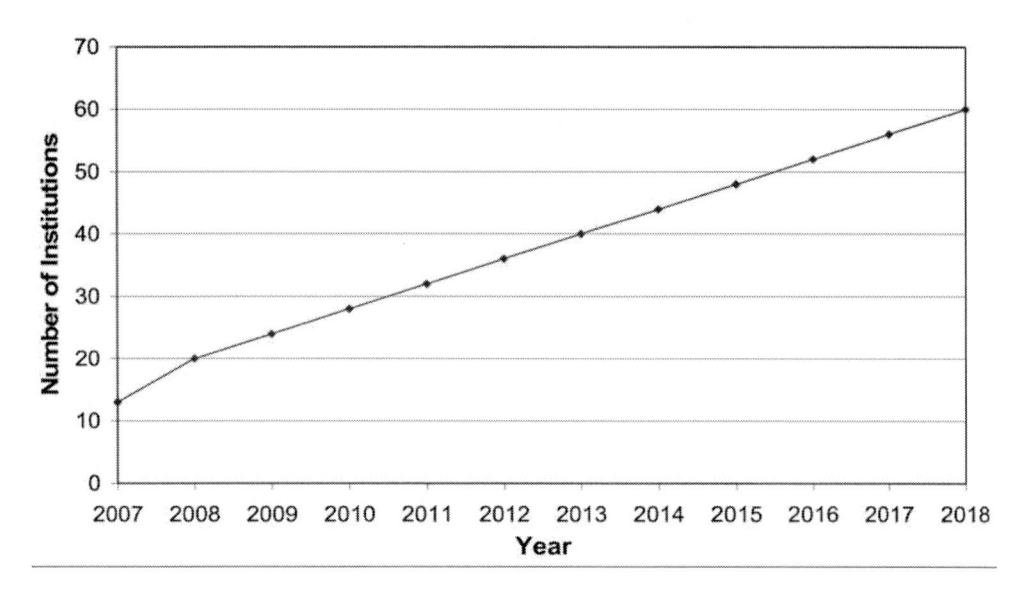

Chart 3. Number of Flagship Institutions by 2018

Flagship Centers at Ohio State University, University of Oregon, and University of Texas, Austin, led the effort to develop the Roadmaps. With funding provided by the U.S. Congress the initiative began in June 2007 with three separate State Language Summits followed by a series of state-level working groups. The effort was overseen by the National Security Education Program with co-sponsorship from the Departments of Defense, Commerce, and Labor. The six-month project culminated in October with the publication of three separate Language Roadmaps for the States of Ohio, Oregon and Texas.

The 2007 Language Roadmaps represent an important recognition by states that they need to clearly articulate the demand for foreign language skills in the broader context of public and private interests. The Roadmap effort seeks to explore the forces involved at state and local levels that create a demand for a 21st-century workforce with demonstrated proficiencies in foreign languages and international cultural knowledge. It also seeks to more precisely define the roles of federal and state governments, the education community (including K-12 and higher education teachers, administrators, and parents), and business in moving forward with strategic plans that put important programs and initiatives in place.

**Building the Roadmaps**

Content for the Roadmaps was developed by working groups after intensive Language Summits held in Columbus, Ohio; Portland, Oregon; and Austin, Texas. The objective of each Summit was to "map" the demand for foreign language in the state. Government and business representatives were actively engaged in articulating the demand side, while educators from K-12, state boards of education, and universities represented the supply side. The Summit agenda focused on a "think tank" environment where the participants discussed the factors that either drive or inhibit the capacity of the state to address the need for foreign language and international education.

Following the Summit, each project convened a series of working groups composed of representatives from business, state and local government, and education. The challenge to these working groups was to develop a strategic plan that would reflect the economic, political, and social realities of the state.

The final product of each group is the *State Roadmap to Language Excellence*. The Roadmaps are designed to provide strategically developed proposals that help implement short- and longterm approaches to foreign language and cultural education in the state system. Each of the Language Roadmaps establishes an independent set of goals and timelines for implementation; however, they share common themes.

## Language and Public Policy

The Language Roadmap process introduced language education as an important element of the public policy debate, asking state policymakers and business leaders to examine their priorities and seek ways to identify the needs for a workforce with these skills. The engagement of state and local government decision makers and the business community has served as an important and necessary step in moving the language agenda forward. Flagship Centers will continue to explore efforts to address key components of the Roadmap and to facilitate opportunities for additional states to develop their own Roadmaps.

## Establishing Advocacy and Coordination at the State Level

Each Roadmap calls for the establishment of an office or organization whose mission is to take primary responsibility for the issue. Oregon proposes the development of an office that would assist the Oregon Department of Education in its effort to provide leadership to expand dual language programs and international exchanges, guidance for proficiency development and assessment, state proficiency goals and support language teacher licensures. Ohio proposes a center to reside either in an appropriate government agency, an institution of higher education, or as an independent non-profit organization. Texas acknowledges that a high-level coordinating board must be legally mandated to establish benchmarks and assess the state's performance in reaching the core objectives of the effort.

## Teacher Certification

Each Roadmap recognizes that a severely limiting factor in expansion of language learning is the lack of qualified and certified teachers and instructors. More accelerated teacher training programs for high-need critical languages are needed. A number of approaches are recommended:

- Coordinating teacher incentive programs to provide scholarships for language-proficient students to pursue teaching careers.
- Encouraging bilingual individuals seeking certification in other content areas to help staff dual language and immersion program.
- Recruiting college-educated heritage speakers to become licensed teachers

## Language Learning and Academic Performance: Public Awareness

The Roadmaps acknowledge in the past decade several developments that have detracted from the ability to implement language programs in elementary, middle and high school. There is evidence of an entrenched bias toward English and a pervasive idea that English in the only language needed for business. Each of the Roadmaps includes an imperative for the development and implementation of outreach strategies.

### Start Language Learning Early

Each Roadmap identifies the key to producing proficient language users is to start learning early and continue it as a life-long endeavor. The Oregon Roadmap offers a new approach characterized by benefits for students with language proficiency. The system will reward students and educational institutions that succeed, rather than punishing those who fail and by creating an environment that encourages reform rather than mandating reform. Programs of scholarship support to those who are willing to pursue careers in teaching languages and high school and college credit to students with demonstrated language performance are included in the Oregon Roadmap. The Texas Roadmap advocates an Early Start Initiative representing a partnership among school districts, higher education, parents, business and local communities to establish pre-K programs following established early language learning models.

### Moving Forward

The Roadmaps to Language Excellence serve as a source of important ideas and strategies, not only for Ohio, Oregon and Texas, but for states and the federal sector. Flagship Centers will remain an integral component of the Roadmap implementation phase and will continue to seek ways to expand the reach of innovative approaches and best practices throughout the U.S. During 2008 we have worked closely with the Office of the Governor of Utah to structure their internally funded state roadmap effort. We have also identified a number of additional states that have indicated interest in advancing their own strategic planning efforts.

## NATIONAL LANGUAGE SERVICE CORPS

## Background

The NLSC (initially called the "Civilian Linguist Reserve Corps") is both a major component of the Department of Defense plan to address future surge requirements and the National Security Language Initiative whose objectives is to build national capacity.

The Intelligence Authorization Act for Fiscal Year 2005 (Public Law 108-487), Section 613, authorized the Director of National Intelligence to conduct a three-year pilot project to assess the feasibility and advisability of establishing a Civilian Linguist Reserve Corps.

In January 2006, the creation of a "Language Corps" became an integral component of the President's National Security Language Initiative (NSLI). The goal of NSLI is to enhance national well-being through increasing our foreign language capabilities. The Department of Defense embraced the concept of a "Language Corps" and proposed the implementation of the "Language Corps" concept as an integral component of its Language Transformation Plan and its role in NSLI. The John Warner National Defense Authorization Act for Fiscal Year 2007, transferred the administration of the pilot project to the Secretary of Defense.

NLSC pilot implementation is now assigned to the Department of Defense (Office of the Secretary of Defense/Personnel & Readiness) with program responsibility for implementing the program assigned to the Director, National Security Education Program (NSEP).

Foreign language skills are recognized as critical to the security and well-being of the nation. These skills are essential to the capacity of the federal sector to respond to national and international needs, particularly those that arise during national and international threats, emergencies, and disasters. The National Language Service Corps represents the first organized national attempt to capitalize on our rich national diversity in language and culture.

The federal government cannot reasonably be expected to possess the wide range of language capabilities that may be necessary to address immediate or emergency surge requirements. The National Language Service Corps (NLSC) is designed to address the need for surge language capabilities by providing and maintaining a readily available civilian corps of certified expertise in languages determined to be important to the security and welfare of the nation. The Corps is established as a public organization that, upon becoming fully operational, will fill gaps that inevitably exist between requirements and available language skills. In addition, it is designed to provide the capabilities for meeting short-, mid-, and long-term requirements through the identification and warehousing of expertise and skills in current and potential critical languages. These language capabilities serve the broader interests of the federal departments and their agencies. Over the longer-term such capabilities might also serve the interests of state and local governments. The NLSC will maintain a roster of individuals with certified language skills who are readily available in time of war, national emergency, or other national needs. The design for the NLSC builds on and complements the solid baseline of capabilities established in other existing programs. The NLSC will adopt and will make use of the best practices, efficiencies, and cost effectiveness of appropriate civilian and military reserve models as well as the models of other organizations.

The NLSC will be comprised of United States citizens who are highly proficient in English as well as one or more foreign languages. These individuals would agree to offer their certified language skills in support of federal agencies responding to domestic or foreign disasters and other-than-emergency activities for the security and welfare of the nation. The National Language Service Corps will offer language-competent individuals the opportunity to support government efforts, particularly during times of emergencies or crises when their expertise can truly make a difference.

The NLSC effort is designed as a pilot allowing a team of experts to examine, in a costeffective manner, all of the complexities involved in developing a complex organization. Having completed the first of its three year pilot, the NLSC has: (1) developed its concept of operations that have been vetted through a wide range of federal organizations; (2) established necessary capabilities; (3) assembled the correct team; (4) established strong interest among a wide range of federal departments and agencies of the executive branch; and (5) through extensive research and outreach efforts, established public interest in serving. During the coming year, in the second phase of its operation, the NLSC will implement all key components of the pilot in order to test and refine the process.

The goal of the NLSC pilot project is to create a cadre of at least 1000 highly proficient members in 10 languages by 2010.

## The NLSC Concept

The NLSC represents a vital new approach to address the nation's needs for individuals with highly developed language skills. Focus group research undertaken by nationally recognized marketing and branding experts revealed a strong motivation on the part of Americans to serve not only the nation but their states and local communities. This research also led to the change in name from "Civilian Linguist Reserve Corps" to "National Language Service Corps" in an effort to maximize the appeal of the organization to the broadest population.

NLSC members represent a national asset to support the nation's emergency responders when they must communicate with local populations during times of need. The nation will draw on NLSC members to address homeland and national security requirements as well as international emergency and relief efforts. Ideally, state and local users will also have the capacity to draw from a common pool of NLSC members for temporary and/or part-time assistance.

## Concept of Operations

The NLSC is a pilot organization that is civilian in nature and operates in a civilian environment. Its members must be U.S. citizens who are at least 18 years old. In addition to the general population, potential recruiting pools include students and faculty at colleges and universities, retired military personnel, retired and former federal employees, and volunteers in already existing programs such as AmeriCorps, Senior Corps, and Learn and Serve America.

NLSC members voluntarily join and renew their membership in an organization that considers and adapts the best practices of volunteer organizations. Certified NLSC members are organized into National Pool and Dedicated Sponsor Pools. These members volunteer to be registered in a national database and are typically given an assignment by the NLSC upon a request from a federal sponsor for service. The two pools provide the requesting agency with a choice of options that best match their requirements and expectations.

The National Pool consists of a broader array of talent that will be warehoused and maintained to be drawn upon by all federal agencies during times of need. The primary focus of this group is to meet unanticipated and/or surge requirements for language skills. In a broad sense, members of the National Pool provide language expertise as required for short-term situations that do not require significant job-related training to support a particular organization. These individuals are, in many ways, similar to "temporary" employees and may be provided compensation for their services. Members of the National Pool also have the option of joining the Dedicated Sponsor Pool, and vice versa.

The Dedicated Sponsor Pool is a group of individuals who agree to provide recurring support to a federal organization by habitually performing duties requiring specific language and potentially professional skills in support of a sponsoring USG organization or agency. This agreement may include performing responsibilities and duties for a declared number of days of service per year as well as a requirement to either use existing or sponsor-provided professional or technical skills in addition to the language skills for which they are primarily needed. The Dedicated Sponsor Pool provides a major source of trusted personnel augmentation with professional and specialized language skills to develop and support long-term sustainability of close and mutually beneficial relationships. Its members are readily available for designated periods of service and provide dependable job performance and language expertise to the sponsor. This long-term relationship and commitment contributes to an enduring relationship that builds mutual confidence and improves both efficiency and effectiveness. It is envisioned that the Dedicated Sponsor Pool will have fewer members than the National Pool since it is tailored to satisfy specific, identified requirements.

The languages of interest to the NLSC reflect short- and long-term requirements with emphasis on expertise critical not only to national security but to the needs and requirements of a broad array of federal agencies. While the pilot NLSC will address a smaller subset of languages, we envision the fully implemented organization will address a very wide array of languages, perhaps more than 150 languages. The number of members associated with each language will ultimately be based upon the priorities and needs of the agencies of the Federal Government.

It is generally desirable for NLSC members to possess Level 3 language proficiency or higher in all modalities – reading, writing, speaking, and listening, as defined on the Interagency Language Roundtable (ILR) scale. The NLSC will maintain a database of individuals who have some measurable skills in less common languages but who do not meet the Level 3 language proficiency. These individuals may be contacted when a requirement develops.

The NLSC will conduct assessments and certify the language skill proficiency levels of its members. This responsibility includes conducting performance-based testing, which leverages available resources for testing languages of interest, as the central component of the certification process. Similar efforts will be made in determining the availability of satisfactory tests in the other priority languages. The Dedicated Sponsor is responsible for providing job skills and sustaining language skill training for members of this pool.

The NLSC will leverage technology in a 24/7 Operations Support Center that will represent a key function for maintaining the Corps. This Center is expected to evolve into the information, communication, data, member readiness training, and operational hub for the Corps. Through the 24/7 Operations Support Center, the NLSC uses available resources to support language proficiency sustainment and certification of its Members.

The NLSC reaches out to the various populations with a targeted requirements-based marketing and recruiting strategy to enroll members. The NLSC is devising an operational plan that will provide direct interface with federal agencies to assist them, where necessary, in identifying their language skill requirements. This analysis will help identify gaps between existing language skills and the number of linguists available as input data for developing targeted recruiting and marketing goals and strategies.

The NLSC will be proactive in placing members in positions of service across the Federal Government. The NLSC will maintain up-to-date information on all members. The NLSC will recruit, certify, enroll, train, and maintain National and Dedicated Sponsor Pool members consistent with supported organization requirements. When approved requests for language support are received, the appropriate NLSC member(s) will be assigned and provide service as federal employees on temporary duty (TDY) to support the requesting agency.

NLSC support will be provided to all departments and agencies of the USG and, when authorized, to state and local governments. The requesting agency and the NLSC will utilize memorandum of agreements to establish the relationships, and the roles and responsibilities of the parties. At a minimum, agreements will identify the requesting agency's language requirements.

The Concept of Operations supports the concept of the NLSC as a public civilian organization to fill gaps in language requirements and capabilities across federal departments and agencies. It is composed of members who are motivated, prepared, and on-call to use their language skills to help others by providing surge language support for federal departments and agencies, particularly during national crises/emergencies.

NLSC members may be assigned as intermittent Federal employees when requested by a federal agency and may be physically moved as members of a government response team to provide on-site language support, including locations OCONUS.

Duty assignments of NLSC members may be based upon language skills and, potentially, occupational skills sets with the opportunities for service varying from emergency relief to international crises to immediate national need—wherever language skills are needed. Members of the Corps will be compensated for their services when activated. They also will receive a significant personal reward from knowing that their power to communicate across languages and cultures has contributed to a deeper understanding among all nations.

The NLSC prepares its members for assignments as a member of a government team in support of federal departments and agencies. The preparation of its members includes an understanding of the working culture of the organization being supported. The NLSC engages and interacts with its enrolled members on a regular basis to maintain their interest and involvement. It also supports language proficiency sustainment and enhancement, and provides resources for professional opportunities in language. The NLSC Concept of Operations does not include language training, but links to resources for language training will be provided to NLSC Members.

## Accomplishments

The U.S. Government awarded a competitive contract in April 2007 to General Dynamics Information Technology as the prime contractor to conduct a three-year pilot NLSC program. The pilot is overseen by the National Security Education Program (NSEP) at the Department of Defense. The pilot program started in mid April, 2007, with a team of nationally recognized experts developing the Concept of Operations for a prototype NLSC. The accomplishments of the NLSC Team during Phase 1 of the prototype include:

- Conducting a Proof of Principle of the NLSC through a series of interactive functional exercises carefully designed to provide details for their performance, organizational structure, and metrics for measuring and reporting their progress to support preparing a Concept of Operations for each function.
- Developing a NLSC Concept of Operations (CONOPS) that guides the establishment and evaluation of the pilot NLSC. It represents the best ideas produced through a series of functional workshops that included representatives of the federal and state organizations that are the expected beneficiaries of the NLSC. Functions were further evaluated as integrated processes in Capstone exercises that included additional representatives from the same communities. The result is an initial NLSC CONOPS that is comprehensive, complete and preliminarily vetted with the User community.

- Preparing the NLSC Marketing and Recruiting Plan with a methodology for locating and attracting prospective NLSC member volunteers while providing internal guidance to recruiters and marketers. This methodology includes determining marketing and recruiting objectives, defining a target market and developing enrollment quotas. Additionally, the Plan summarizes a process to develop metrics and assist recruiters and marketers by helping them to optimize the marketing and recruiting tools at their disposal.
- Developing and delivering an NLSC logo that conveys a message of service through the use of a colorful weave design. The expressed message is one of diversity illustrating that speakers of foreign languages can use their skills working together for the good of others.
- Creating the NLSC tagline that conveys the message to speakers of foreign languages that their ability to communicate in a language other than English can be used to help other people.
- Developing the NLSC Language Proficiency Certification Plan that focuses on the testing methods and requirements to certify individuals in designated languages.
- Preparing the preliminary Compensation Plan for NLSC members appointed temporary employees in the Federal Government on an intermittent work schedule.
- Developing a preliminary Contract Plan (terms of service/employment) for NLSC members that includes identification of documents and forms required to legally record agreements and actions between NLSC and its members, clients, and suppliers.
- Preparing the Preliminary Report on Legislative Requirements for a permanent NLSC.
- Conducting outreach to key language constituencies to develop long term relationships.
- Facilitating marketing, advertising, recruiting, certification, community relations, public relations, NLSC member professional development, and other NLSC functions.

## Next Steps

During the remaining phases of the prototype, the NLSC Team will test and evaluate the NLSC Concepts of Operations (CONOPS), the functions to be performed, and the organizational structure to provide data for preparing the plan for a fully operational organization. This effort includes recruiting and enrolling 1000 members with competency in ten languages important to national security and the welfare of the nation. The test and evaluation will further develop and mature the Prototype during a series of scenario-driven staff exercises and activation exercises as the primary vehicles for testing and evaluating the integrated CONOPS.

The first activation exercise is planned to be with the Center for Disease Control (CDC) responding to an emergency environment located in the United States. If possible, the activation will be part of a regularly-scheduled CDC exercise. The second activation exercise is planned to be with the DoD Pacific Command (PACOM) and will activate and deploy

NLSC members to locations outside the United States. This exercise will include NLSC operations under normal conditions. The third activation exercise is planned to be with the Defense Intelligence Agency operating at a location within the United States in a non-emergency scenario. These activation exercises provide opportunities to explore, test, validate, and provide feedback for adapting the CONOPS and business practices under circumstances and environments that approximate real-world conditions. During each exercise, the NLSC plans to alert 100 members, activate 50 members, and physically deploy and redeploy 5 members as part of an integrated government team. These activations will provide data for each data element and each measure of performance comprising the metrics for NLSC operations. The Director of NSEP is coordinating the participation of federal agencies as partners for the Prototype.

The NLSC will continue outreach to national, regional, and local ethnic heritage communities, organizations of language professionals, US Government retirees, and academic institutions and associations in order to establish long-term relationships. These interactions will help the NLSC facilitate recruiting from these segments of the population as well as expand the professional development and language proficiency certification opportunities open to the NLSC and its members.

These activities of the NSEP demonstrate that the Department of Defense is committed to expanding the language capacity of our nation. Our national security demands these skills. We continue to aggressively encourage the state, federal, business, and academic sectors to join us in this critical undertaking.

## END NOTE

[1] The target proficiency is Interagency Language Roundtable (ILR) Level 3 or the American Council for the Teachers of Foreign Languages (ACTFL) Superior Level.

In: Building Strategic Language Ability Programs
Editor: Joshua R. Weston

ISBN: 978-1-60741-127-7
© 2010 Nova Science Publishers, Inc.

*Chapter 5*

# THE BRIGHAM YOUNG UNIVERSITY CHINESE FLAGSHIP PROGRAM AND ITS ROLE IN THE UTAH FOREIGN LANGUAGE ENVIRONMENT: STATEMENT OF DANA S. BOURGERIE BEFORE THE HOUSE ARMED SERVICES COMMITTEE, SUBCOMMITTEE ON OVERSIGHT AND INVESTIGATIONS

## I. INTRODUCTION AND BACKGROUND

Mr. Chairman and members of this distinguished committee, thank you for the opportunity to speak with you about the Brigham Young University's National Chinese Flagship Center and its relationship to the larger NSEP Flagship initiative,

You have requested that I focus on the work done within the Brigham Young University (BYU) Flagship Center and its impact on the State of Utah's language environment.

Every year many thousands of students from countries across the world arrive at US institutions of higher learning. While many come specifically to learn English, many others come as matriculating students in undergraduate programs, graduate programs, and in other programs, eventually attaining degrees along side their American counterparts. In doing so, they attain high levels of English, knowledge of American culture, and its institutions.

By contrast, although Americans have been studying abroad in increasing numbers since the 1960s, few enroll as regular students or attain the kind of language proficiency and cultural knowledge that would allow them to function professionally in the way their foreign counterparts do in the US. Instead, most enroll in "protected" language courses with students from their own institutions or their own country. This deficiency is the norm in languages designated as critical to US interests such as Chinese, Arabic, Russian, Hindi/Urdu, and others that are part of The Language Flagship group. Indeed, Americans obtaining a professional level of language proficiency is rare enough that when it does occur it often warrants special media attention in the overseas locales where the individual is residing. Our

Flagship students are routinely written up in Chinese newspapers as outstanding examples of language learners because of their ability to speak Chinese in professional situations.

This media attention is flattering to our students and to our programs and is in fact tangible evidence of the Flagships' success in training students. At the same time it highlights how far we as a nation still need to go in developing the kind of professionals and specialists that are critical to fostering and protecting our national interests. The strategic imbalance inherent in the gap in foreign language abilities of American students compared to the English abilities of those from other countries is remarkable, and is evident in both business and government.

Allow me to share a personal example. Last year I was contacted by a law firm, which was representing a US capitol investment company negotiating a contract with Chinese and Thai partners worth hundreds of millions of dollars. Among the Chinese Thai partners were at least a half dozen individuals who had degrees (many advanced degrees) from the US, who had lived many years in the US, and who were well versed in American cultural practices and negotiating techniques. And, of course, many had excellent English language skills, using interpreters for strategic reasons only. On the American side, there was not a single Chinese speaker or anyone who had accumulated more than a few weeks of experience in China and Thailand. The Americans were even relying on the opposite side's interpreter to help them bridge the language barrier, and until the last stages of the contract, the American side failed to see their situation as problematic. Finally, I was asked to come in and help fix an impasse in completing the negotiations.

The Flagship programs are designed to address just these kinds of imbalances and to disseminate and diffuse practices that would allow institutions beyond its direct scope to similarly train American students to operate professionally in their language of interest. Although the Flagship focus is on designated critical languages, it is hoped that its influence will be much wider, affecting the field of language teaching as a whole. After only seven years of operation, there is strong evidence that this change is happening.

The remainder of my remarks will outline what is being done in the BYU Chinese Flagship program that relate to national Flagship efforts and that support language learning initiatives in the State of Utah.

## II. WHAT IS THE FLAGSHIP INITIATIVE?

The Language Flagship initiative, which began relatively modestly in 2002 with four participating institutions, seeks to produce global professionals in strategic languages with Superior (ILR 3/3+) language skills through a government-academic partnership. In less than seven years, The Language Flagship has now grown to include twelve domestic Flagship centers, seven overseas Flagship centers, six Flagship partner programs, and three K-12 Flagship programs, which as a group are teaching African languages, Arabic, Chinese, Hindi/Urdu, Korean, Persian, Russian, and Central Asian Turkic languages. Most Flagship programs focus on instruction in the upper range of the ACTFL and ILR proficiency scales and aim to create global professionals for government, business, industry, and education.

Although each Flagship program has its local context and language-specific challenges, all are tied together by a common set of principles and features. Each program is a part of a larger collaborative system, which is committed to:

- Providing students with the linguistic and cultural skills necessary to become global professionals.
- Using an assessment system that includes standardized tests and portfolios.

At the heart of the Flagship movement is recognition that high linguistic proficiency alone is insufficient to meet the growing demands placed on professionals working in increasingly sophisticated international markets and government roles. Along with the linguistic proficiency goal of ACTFL Superior (ILR 3/3+), students must develop cultural knowledge and specific domain knowledge to become true global professionals. Most Flagship programs make use of domain language training, advanced cultural training, direct enrollment in target-country universities, and internships to help students achieve these complementary goals.

In a broader sense, The Language Flagship seeks to change the way languages are taught in the U.S. by infusing universities with the kind of model of advanced learning, which can be used to build capacity in critical languages and, eventually, in all languages. Each Flagship follows this general model to pursue a shared mission of creating global professionals, but each does so by leveraging local resources and collaborating with local partners.

## The Chinese Flagship Group

There are currently seven Chinese Flagship programs located in the U.S., and each has a somewhat different designation and charge:

- Brigham Young University Chinese Flagship Center (undergraduate post-baccalaureate corticated)
- The University of Mississippi Chinese Flagship Center (undergraduate)
- The Ohio State University Chinese Flagship Center (K-16)
- The University of Oregon Chinese Flagship Center (K-16)
- Arizona State University Chinese Partner Program
- Indiana University Chinese Partner Program (2008)
- University of Rhode Island Chinese Partner Program (2008)

These seven domestic programs are supported by two overseas Chinese Flagship Centers:

- Nanjing University Chinese Flagship Center (BYU administered)
- Qingdao Chinese Flagship Center (OSU administered)

Two overseas centers serve the needs of all domestic Chinese programs:
The domestic curricula of Flagship programs vary, though most operate as undergraduate programs. Among the Chinese programs, The Ohio State University Flagship program is the

only one to offer both an undergraduate option and a master's degree. Brigham Young University's Flagship is an undergraduate program, but offers a certificate for a limited number of post-baccalaureate students. Whereas Brigham Young University typically accepts students in the junior or senior year, the University of Oregon operates as a four-year program. Two of the Chinese centers (Ohio State University and the University of Oregon) are designated as K-16 centers charged with developing articulated K-16 models leading to superior proficiency.

All of the domestic Chinese Flagship programs culminate with an overseas capstone experience, which includes direct enrollment at Nanjing University and internships managed by the Qingdao center. The overseas capstone experience in China requires students to operate in Chinese academic and workplace cultures – thus simulating their future roles as professionals working in Chinese-speaking contexts. Unlike traditional study abroad programs where students primarily enroll in protected courses designed for foreigners, the Nanjing Center facilitates enrollment in regular courses at Chinese universities that match the students' domain interests or college majors. They are also required to complete internships and/or community service experiences in China to provide experiential learning opportunities.

## III. THE BRIGHAM YOUNG UNIVERSITY FLAGSHIP MODEL

### Purpose and Goals of the BYU Program

In line with the general goals of the Flagship program, the BYU program has as a core focus the training of students to operate professionally in the Chinese language, domestically and internationally. Our mission statement captures that aim.

*The Chinese Flagship Program seeks to prepare students for careers related to China. The Program's aim is to provide participants with the linguistic, cultural, and professional skills necessary to realize their professional goals within a Chinese environment.*

All of what we do is with this mission in mind and each phase of the program is designed to take the student to that stated level. Attaining this single goal requires a multifaceted curriculum, which addresses several integrated supporting objectives:

- Raise general proficiency scores from ACTFL Advanced Plus ( ILR 2/2+) to Superior (ILR 3/3+)
- Increase capabilities in specialized professional communication tasks.
- Provide general and domain-related cultural training.
- Add value to existing un iversity preparation and previous language experience.

### Institutional Context of the BYU Chinese Flagship Center

In its seventh year of operation, the Brigham Young University Flagship Center is a collaborative activity, which is integrated into the Department of Asian and Near Eastern

Languages, and which receives additional administrative support from the university's Center for Language Studies. Both the language department and the Center are units of the College of Humanities. The Department of Asian and Near Eastern Languages' Chinese program is among the largest in the U.S. with annual enrollments of around 1,600, and the program continues to grow. The department has seven full-time Chinese language faculty; three long-term, part-time instructors; and numerous student instructors. The Flagship Center benefits from support from other key campus units, including the Kennedy Center for International Studies, the International Students Programs Office, the Global Management Center at the Marriott School of Business, and the Department of Education supported National Middle Eastern Resource Center.

Although the general public does not always associate Utah with international activities or with ethnic diversity, the area has a significant minority population – especially in the large population centers along the "Wasatch Front" where BYU is located.[1] The Salt Lake City area is also home to one of ten national refugee relocation centers in the United States. Utah's Asian population is around 2% (compared to 4% nationally). Despite the relatively low minority population in much of the state, Utah is rich with international experience. Over 60% of Utahans affiliate with the Church of Jesus Christ of Latter Day Saints (also referred to as the Mormon Church or the LDS church), whose worldwide headquarters are located in Salt Lake City. The widespread tradition among young LDS church members to serve throughout the world as volunteer missionaries has contributed to a high level of international interest in the state. BYU and other higher education institutions enroll large numbers of former missionaries with overseas residence and language experience. As a result, BYU has among the highest number of second language speakers in the nation, with more than 77% of the student body (85% of the seniors) reporting that they speak a second language.[2] Moreover, this tradition of language learning extends beyond the LDS population, and interest in language learning is strong across the state.

## Recruitment and Admissions

The BYU Chinese program is among the largest in the country, and likely enrolls more non-heritage Chinese learners than any other university. The BYU Chinese Flagship Program draws heavily from its regular Chinese program, but also recruits nationally. Each year, about a fourth of the entering Flagship students come from outside the university.

Because of the strength of BYU's lower-division Chinese program, the Flagship program is able to rely on those courses to teach foundation language skills and then admit students no earlier than their junior year. While the percentage of heritage students enrolled is smaller than at many of the urban centers in the US, the number is still significant at an estimated 15%. Among the forty-two students who have participated in the program, seven have been heritage learners and about half have been former missionaries from Chinese-speaking areas. The remainder of the students has been traditional learners, who began studying in regular courses. Most have had substantial experience with another foreign language and participated in traditional study abroad programs at least once. We have also had student returnees from other service programs such as the Peace Corps.

Importantly, BYU does not limit recruitment to Chinese majors, but looks for students with clear professional goals in any field. Many recruits are "double majors" who are meeting the requirements for a major in Chinese and another professional field. The most common fields have been accounting, business, economics, engineering, and international relations. Other less commonly chosen fields have included journalism, microbiology, pre-med, and visual arts.

BYU has reached out to other higher education institutions through contacts with their language departments and their advisement centers. The University of Utah and Utah State University represent particularly good recruiting sources for the BYU program since both have similar student demographics. Nationally, BYU has used Chinese language associations' networks to advertise its program. Applicants from the national pool are typically students seeking certificates as special status, post-baccalaureate students. Besides BYU, we have had successful applicants from The University of Texas, Duke, Notre Dame, U.C, Irvine, Arkansas, the University of New Hampshire, The University of Georgia, the University of Maryland, the University of Florida, University of Colorado, Penn State University, the University of Hawaii, among others.

## The Structure and Pedagogical Approach of the BYU Advanced Program

Although BYU recruits students in their freshman year and, increasingly, in the K-12 sector, the BYU program does not formally admit students until at least the junior year of college. The BYU lower-division language courses have the goal of building the students' general language skills, and the Flagship program can then select from that strong pool of applicants when admitting students into the advanced program. After admission to the Flagship program, the pedagogical focus shifts to domain specific and content-based work.

The Flagship program does not have a one-size fits all program. Rather there are multiple tracks available, which provide the flexibility necessary to meet the needs of learners with different experience and competency profiles. The flexibility provided by the different program tracks is complemented by a closely articulated course sequence within each track. Tables 2 and 3 show the various tracks(and the content of those tracks) available to participants of the BYU Flagship program.

The BYU program is not only designed for flexibility in terms of entry point but also for accommodating the great variability in student background that is typically found in highlevel language training. BYU Flagship's curriculum is among the most individualized of all the Flagship programs in that the core of the special-purpose coursework is organized around a set of one-on-one tutorials and small group work.

Another advantage of the individualized instruction in the BYU Chinese Flagship program is that it accommodates a large number of domain interests. Because it cannot be expected that the language instructors will also be specialists in every one of the students' domain areas, BYU handles this challenge by using an array of native-speaking Chinese graduate student tutors who are trained to help students learn about the specialty language and practice of their common field of interest. The BYU Flagship also makes use of target language content recitation sections attached to regular courses taught in English. For example, we have convened a twice weekly, small group course attached to an existing China Political Science course, but which is conducted in Chinese. This strategy is similar to the Languages Across the Curriculum approach used at some institutions in the US. To date, the technical domains that the students have woven into their Chinese instruction include:

- Accounting
- Business
- Chemistry
- Development
- Economics
- Engineering
- Environmental issues
- International Studies
- Journalism
- Law
- Marketing
- Political Science
- Public Health
- Public Relations

## IV. K-12 PARTNERSHIPS AND PROGRAM ARTICULATION IN UTAH

As is the case throughout the U.S., Chinese enrollments have burgeoned in Utah in the last five years. Although still a small percentage of total foreign language enrollments, the number of students studying Chinese in Utah has grown substantially from 183 in 2003 to 1215 in 2007 (see Table 1 below), with a projected enrollment between 3000- 3500 in 2008.

### Table 1. Chinese Enrollments from 2003 through 2007 (Secondary Student Only Grades 7–12)[3]

| Lan-guage | Year | | | | | | | | | |
|---|---|---|---|---|---|---|---|---|---|---|
| | 2003 | | 2004 | | 2005 | | 2006 | | 2007 | |
| | *Count* | *Pct* | *Count* | *Pct* | *Count* | *Pct* | *Count* | *Pct* | Count | Pct |
| Chi-nes e | 183 | 0.25% | 159 | 0.24 % | 263 | 0.39% | 435 | 0.61% | 1215 | 1.54 % |
| Total | 73983 | 100% | 65409 | 100% | 68258 | 100% | 71602 | 100% | 78878 | 100% |

Source: Utah Department of Education, World Language Office

### Table 2. BYU Chinese Flagship Track Options

| Track | Duration | Description |
|---|---|---|
| Junior Track | 3 Years | For Intermediate/Intermediate-High students who still need to complete substantial major work and upper-level general Chinese training (e.g., media Chinese, literary Chinese, and literature survey). Restricted to matriculating BYU students. |
| Senior Track | 2 Years | For students who have largely completed their majors and who can devote most of their time to Flagship-specific study. |
| Fast Track | 1 Year | For candidates entering at a minimum of ACTFL Advanced (ILR 2+/3) and have already completed upper-level cultural and linguistic training. Ideal for at-large candidates who have done other substantial study outside of BYU. |

**Table 3. Content Overview of the Instructional Tracks within the BYU Flagship Program**

| Academic Year | | Sep | Oct | Nov | Dec | Jan | Feb | Mar | Apr | May | Jun | Jul | Aug |
|---|---|---|---|---|---|---|---|---|---|---|---|---|---|
| **JUNIOR TRACK** | Y1 | Advanced Chinese Major course work Specialty advisement | | | | Advanced Chinese Major course work Specialty advisement | | | | Optional Flagship Major courses | | | |
| | Y2 | Domain and content training | | | | Domain and content training | | | | | | | |
| | Y3 Overseas | Direct enrollment in Nanjing | | | | Internship in China | | | | | | | |
| **SENIOR TRACK/ Special status post-BA** | Y1 | Domain and content training | | | | Domain and content training Culture course | | | | Domain and content training | | | |
| | Y2 Overseas | Direct enrollment in Nanjing | | | | Internship in China | | | | | | | |
| **FAST TRACK (1 Year)** | | Domain and content training | | | | Direct enrollment in Nanjing Culture course | | | | Internship in China | | | |

In 2003, fewer than six high school Chinese programs in Utah existed. In 2008, there will be seventy-four secondary school programs. Moreover, there will be ten Chinese dual language immersion programs beginning in Utah for the 2009–10 school year in six different school districts (Alpine, Davis, Granite, Jordan, Provo, and Weber). Two more school districts (Park City and Salt Lake City) will join the immersion group in 2010–11. Two state bills, which passed with bipartisan support, have funded nearly all of this recent growth:

- SB 80 (2007) Critical Language Program: $330,000 per year for six years for critical language programs in secondary schools.
- SB 41 (2008) Critical Language Program: $480,000 per year for six years for critical language programs in secondary schools and $280,000 for critical dual language programs in elementary schools (Chinese, French, Spanish) per year for six years.

These state-based incentives have allowed the BYU Flagship to focus on curriculum development, assessment support, and teacher training and to use recently allocated K-12 linkage funds to respond to specific requests from the World Languages Unit at the Utah Department of Education and from individual districts.

Two BYU Flagship Center sponsored efforts include the Chinese EDNET distance program for high schools and a STARTALK Program (http://startalk.umd.edu), which includes both a K-12 intensive Chinese language camp and an associated teacher training workshop.

Now in its second year, EDNET (http://ednet.byu.edu) is serving thirty-four sections of level 1 and level 2 Chinese in 28 high schools. The main component of the blendedlearning course originates from the BYU campus and from the Granite School District in the Salt Valley and is transmitted through a video linkup provided by the Utah Education Network (UEN). An experienced master teacher leads these live and interactive broadcasts, which are recorded for occasional delayed broadcast and possible development as part of independent distance education curriculum. Each classroom has a Chinese-speaking facilitator on-site to support the live lesson and to carry out specifically designed activities. Currently the Chinese EDNET program serves approximately 500 students throughout Utah, both in rural and urban districts. This program allows students to study levels one and two of high school Chinese in districts that currently do not have options for traditional classroom programs. Additionally, the program provides a training ground for future teachers as the classroom facilitators gain experience and exposure to teaching methodology. Several of these facilitators are now working toward alternative licensure and will be able to serve as full-fledged teachers in the future.

For the last two years the BYU Flagship Center has sponsored DoD funded STARTALK programs. STARTALK plays two distinct roles in the BYU Flagship K-12 strategy. STARTALK exposes more students to Chinese earlier and helps bolster high school enrollments through its articulated curriculum. In addition, the program serves as an important recruitment tool for the Flagship program as STARTALK students connect with advanced students who serve as counselors.

In its inaugural 2007 program, the BYU STARTALK program enrolled 18 high school students in Chinese classes and 15 teacher trainees in the teacher development track. The 2008 workshop expanded significantly to serve nearly 60 high school students. Moreover the teacher training component served eighteen secondary teachers and perspective teachers, along with fifteen teachers from China's Hanban (National Office For Teaching Chinese as a Foreign Language). This ongoing professional development workshop series helps address the critical need for qualified teachers by providing a methods course toward alternative certification. Partly as a result of the teacher workshop, the Brigham Young University Chinese Flagship program will now sponsor a Utah Chinese language teachers association, which will be formally organized in October 2008.

In addition to EDNET and STARTALK, the BYU Flagship is working with the university's independent study unit to develop a model course for Chinese. Each of these three efforts are articulated and coordinated in terms of curriculum and credit with regular Chinese programs in Utah, allowing students to move smoothly from one program to another. Thus, the relationship between the state and the BYU Flagship represents a true partnership, and each works in a complementary fashion toward achieving larger state goals.

## Technology and Learning Tools

The Flagship Center takes advantage of resources at its Humanities Technology and Research Support Center (HTRSC), whose resources are among the best in the country. HTRSC provides international satellite links, software development support, testing services, and state-of-the-art lab equipment. Within this support structure, the Flagship Center makes wide use of both commercially developed and locally-developed software programs for learning and teaching Chinese. However, because of the individualized nature of advanced language learning, the Center still develops much of the software needs for learning and testing. We also have compiled on-line corpora for the specialty domain topics chosen by our students. Traditional media (newspapers and broadcast news) are also a large part of our curriculum, though now typically delivered online and via streaming video. Each student is supplied with key on-line learning tools, such as *Keytip, Wenlin,* and *Ziba.* Recently, we have piloted use of "Skype pals," whereby program students are linked to students of similar majors in China via Skype voice/video protocol. Skype has become ubiquitous in China and is often included on business cards. In addition, the Center has compiled a video archive that includes commercial broadcasts and video samples done by our own technical staff to specifically address the needs of individualized instruction. For example, we have a set of professional "backgrounders", wherein Chinese professionals are interviewed about their work and show their work places. These "backgrounders" (which have been created in law, medicine, engineering, journalism, teaching, insurance, government, etc.) expose students to specific linguistic terms associated with their specialties and give cultural insights related to the professional practices of key fields.

## Different Paths to China

All Chinese Flagship programs design their programs with the two components of the overseas capstone experience in mind: Direct enrollment at the BYU-managed Flagship Center at Nanjing University and internship placement through the Qingdao Flagship Center. The domestic domain and cultural training prepares students for direct enrollment in their major courses at Nanjing University and then to complete an internship with a company or institution in China. The direct enrollment phase allows students to study alongside native classmates, which is common in the U.S. but rare for American students in China. Students have a chance to live with a native-speaking roommate with a similar academic background. Thus, students gain experience by studying in a Chinese context and by establishing collegial relationships with future Chinese professionals. The Nanjing Flagship Center also provides support provides courses on in Chinese news media and in advanced writing, two areas we have found critical to the success of our students in the capstone experience. Although these courses are dedicated to Flagship Students, they are taught by regular Nanjing University Flagship faculty from the Journalism Department and the Chinese Department respectively.

Students typically complete internships after the direct enrollment phase. The Ohio State University-managed Qingdao Flagship Center places Flagship students in internships. When possible, the interns are placed in Chinese institutions to allow for maximum exposure to Chinese professional practices. Successful navigation of this overseas capstone experience is the ultimate goal of the Flagship Program. All curriculum and activities leading up to the overseas phase of the program are designed to help meet the challenge of being able to serve as a professionals in within a Chinese speaking cultural environment.

## Assessment and Evaluation

The National Security Education Program, which funds The Language Flagship, has insisted on accountability, and the BYU Chinese Flagship program uses a number of assessment and evaluation tools to demonstrate it is meeting its goals. ACTFL-OPI, the Chinese government HSK, and two computer adaptive tests for listening and reading[4] form the core of the standardized measures for the BYU program. BYU also has made limited use of the Standards-based Measurement of Proficiency (STAMP) developed by the Center for Applied Second Language Studies (CASLS), the parent unit of the University of Oregon Flagship program. When available, the Flagship Program has used the Defense Language Proficiency Test (DLPT), one of the Interagency Language Round Table (ILR) group of tests.

In addition to the various standardized measures, the Flagship program collects qualitative data through program surveys, learning journals, and internship providers' surveys. To better serve the Flagship community and the language field as a whole, the Flagship Center uses the qualitative data and proficiency tests scores for research and formative evaluation.

In addition, because there is much that can not be captured in a standardized test, BYU makes use of language portfolios to display the outcomes of the students' efforts, including student presentations, writing samples, resumes, and linguistic history.

## Collaboration and Cooperation with Other Chinese Flagship Programs

Although Flagship models vary, each program works toward producing professionals who have the linguistic and cultural ability to conduct business in Chinese. A key attribute of the Flagship movement is that each program is part of a larger network that draws upon expertise of its language group and of other Flagship language programs. For example, overseas centers serve all programs, and designated K-16 centers such as Ohio State University and the University of Oregon have developed curricula and expertise for Chinese K-12 programs, which can be shared with other emerging programs in Utah and elsewhere. Moreover, programs share assessment tools and portfolio systems.

## Outcomes for Recent Program Graduates

Since the first group of participants entered the BYU Chinese Flagship program, standardized scores have steadily risen to where the majority of students meet the ACTFL Superior level and HSK, which is the China national proficiency, test, similar to TOEFL in English.

To put these scores in to context, the minimum score for entrance into Chinese University as an undergraduate is level 3–4 for the Sciences and level 5–6 for Arts and Sciences. Graduate programs require a minimum 6 in any field. Thus, all Flagship students so far have met direct enrollment entry standards for universities in China.

Beyond standardized tests, the BYU Flagship Center collects a portfolio of outcome data (video taped presentations, writing samples, etc) and personal background information (Chinese/English resumes, employment statements, etc.).

**Table 4. Standardized Testing Results for BYU Flagship Cohorts 1–4**

| Cohort | HSK | ACTFL-OPI | ILR |
|--------|-----|-----------|-----|
| 1 | Level 9: 1<br>Level 8: 3<br>Level 7: 1<br>Level 6: 1 | Superior: 5<br>Advanced: 1 | Level 3: 3<br>Level 2+:2<br>Level 2:1 |
| 2 | Level 8: 2<br>Level 7: 5<br>Level 6: 3 | Superior: 3<br>Advanced: 8 | Level 3+:2<br>Level 3: 3<br>Level 2+:3 |
| 3 | Level 8: 2<br>Level 7: 3<br>Level 6: 1 | Superior: 6<br>Advanced: 2 | Level 3+: 3<br>Level 3: 3<br>Level 2+: 2 |
| 4 | Level 10:1<br>Level 9: 2<br>Level 8: 6<br>Level 7: 4 | Superior: 7<br>Advanced: 5 | Level 3+: 3<br>Level 3: 6<br>Level 2+: 2 |

## Some BYU Flagship Program Alumni Placements

The BYU Center has now graduated 4 cohorts and many are now in the workforce and in professional schools. Below are some of contexts in which graduates are now working or studying.

- Law School
- China Businesses
- State Department
- Commerce
- Other US Government
- Journalism
- Medical School
- Accounting Firms
- Technology Firms

## V. THE BYU FLAGSHIP CENTER'S INFLUENCE ON THE LANGUAGE FIELD AND LOCAL LANGUAGE ENVIRONMENT

*The Utah Governor's Language Summit.* In addition to the recent, specific collaborations with the State of Utah Department of Education (STARTALK and EDNET), the BYU Chinese Flagship Center has been able to positively affect the language learning environment generally in Utah. The Flagship Center was co-organizer of a Utah Governor's language summit on September 16, 2008. The State took full charge of the summit, collaborating with NSEP, and drawing on their expertise from previous language summits. Moreover, Governor John Huntsman gave his direct support to the effort. As in previous language summits in

Ohio, Texas, and Oregon, the gathering brought together representatives from business, education, industry, and government to begin a dialogue toward a language road map for the State of Utah. Speakers and participants included Governor John Huntsman, Dr. David Chu, and State Senator Howard Stevensen (Cochair, Utah public education appropriations committee and main sponsor of the recent foreign language bills). Other key participants included the head of the Governor's economic development office and the head of the Utah World Trade Center.

Major support came from a number of sponsors including American Express ($5000), the Governor's Committee on Economic Development ($2500), the BYU Marriott School Global Management Center/CIBER ($2500), the Utah State Office of Education ($10,000), as well as the Language Flagship and the BYU Chinese Flagship Center. In additional to direct funding support, many hours were donated by top-level business leaders from the World Trade Center Utah, the Salt Lake City Chamber of Commerce, and the Utah County Chamber of Commerce.

The summit was the first step toward developing a language policy for Utah and brought together previously independent parties together in a productive dialogue on the current language capacity and needs in the state. Smaller working committees are currently being formed to draft a formal statement on language policy based on the outcome of the language summit and follow-up research. These results will be brought forward as recommendations to the Utah International Education (IE) Summit in January 2009. The IE Summit will then integrate the resulting road map into the broader Utah international education plan.

Beyond the state summit, the Chinese Flagship Center has reached out to other universities in the state and begun to form partnerships with institutions, especially the University of Utah through its College of Humanities and Confucius Institute. Regionally, we have begun discussions with colleagues in Arizona and Wyoming to explore ways to diffuse successful models that we have developed for professional language training as well. Key educational leaders from Wyoming and Arizona attended the Utah language summit to gain insights for possible future language summits in their own states. Leaders from ACTFL, Asia Society, NCSSFL and K-12 education were also represented at the language summit as national contributors to the dialogue.

## END NOTES

[1] The 2006 census (http://quickfacts.census.gov/qfd/states/41000.html) places Salt Lake City's Hispanic population at 18.8%, more than the national average of 14.8%. In addition, the Pacific Islander population is just under 2%, African American 1.9%, and Native American 1.3%.

[2] Brigham Young University's Center for Language Studies

[3] These numbers are based on October 1 course enrollment data for each academic year.

[4] Computer-Adaptive Test for Reading Chinese (CATRC), Chinese Computerized Adaptive Listening Comprehension Test (CCALT), and *Hanyu Shuiping Kaoshi* (HSK)

# CHAPTER SOURCES

The following chapters have been previously published:

Chapter 1: This is an edited, reformatted and augmented version of the statement of the Oversight and Investigations Subcommittee during the hearing on the DOD's Work with States, Universities, and Students to Transform the Nation's Foreign Language Capacity, September 23, 2008

Chapter 2: This is an edited, reformatted and augmented version of the statement of Galal Walker, National East Asian Languages Resource Center, The Ohio State University, before the House Armed Services Committee, Subcommittee on Oversight and Investigations, dated September 23, 2008

Chapter 3: This is an edited, reformatted and augmented version of the statement of Terri E. Givens, University of Texas at Austin, before the House Armed Services Committee, Subcommittee on Oversight and Investigations, dated September 23, 2008

Chapter 4: This is an edited, reformatted and augmented version of the statement of Robert O. Slater, National Security Education Program, before the House Armed Services Committee, Subcommittee on Oversight and Intelligence, dated September 23, 2008

Chapter 5: This is an edited, reformatted and augmented version of the statement of Dana S. Bourgerie, the National Chinese Flagship Center at Brigham Young University, before the House Armed Services Committee, Subcommittee on Oversight and Investigations, dated September 23, 2008

# INDEX

## D

## E

## F

## G